NATIONAL QUALIFICATIONS

Higher Still

Higher INTERPRETATION PASSAGES
Model Papers

by

H.J. Davidson

ISBN 0 7169 8014 2
© *H.J. Davidson, 2000.*

ROBERT GIBSON · Publisher
17 Fitzroy Place, Glasgow, G3 7SF.

CONTENTS

MODEL PAPER A 4

MODEL PAPER B 14

MODEL PAPER C 25

MODEL PAPER D 32

MODEL PAPER E 40

MODEL PAPER F 48

MODEL PAPER G 56

MODEL PAPER H 64

COPYING PROHIBITED

Note: This publication is **NOT** licensed for copying under the Copyright Licensing Agency's Scheme, to which Robert Gibson & Sons are not party.

All rights reserved. No part of this publication may be reproduced; stored in a retrieval system; or transmitted in any form or by any means — electronic, mechanical, photocopying, or otherwise — without prior permission of the publisher Robert Gibson & Sons, Ltd., 17 Fitzroy Place, Glasgow, G3 7SF.

INTRODUCTION

These tests are intended as practice for the Higher Still Higher Examination in English, Paper I, the Interpretation paper.

The first two tests use only single passages and answers are provided. They are intended to help you get used to the sort of answers required for A — analysis, U — understanding and E — evaluation.

The first test uses quite a short passage written in rather dramatic English. This gives the opportunity to practise A — analysis and E — evaluation questions which you will not have met quite so frequently at Standard Grade. The second test uses a long passage so that you can get used to the amount of reading required. Both of these tests include the full range of questions and also include a comparison between two paragraphs within each passage.

Answers and marking schemes are provided for each of these tests. They should be looked at after each test has been attempted. They give an indication of what is required by the different types of question. They also give an indication of the detail required to gain good marks.

The other six tests each consist of two passages and questions which add up to 60 marks and they all include a comparison between the two passages.

Model Paper C about Lighthouses is probably slightly easier than the others, and Model Paper H about Biographies is slightly more difficult. Tests D, E, F and G are of a similar standard and are as close as possible to what you might expect in the examination.

HIGHER ENGLISH	**MODEL PAPER A** **Interpretation**	NATIONAL QUALIFICATIONS

Time: 1 hour 30 minutes

You should attempt all questions.

The total value of the Paper is 60 marks.

INTERPRETATION

There is ONE passage and questions.

Read the passage carefully and then answer all the questions which follow. **Use your own words whenever possible and particularly when you are instructed to do so.**

You should read the passage to:

- understand what the author has to say about the sinking of the famous ship the *Titanic* (**Understanding — U**);

- analyse the choice of language, imagery and structures to show how they convey his point of view and contribute to the impact of his description (**Analysis — A**);

- evaluate how effectively he has achieved his purpose (**Evaluation — E**).

A code letter (U, A, E) is used alongside each question to give some indication of the skills being assessed. The number of marks attached to each question will give some indication of the length and kind of answer required.

This extract comes from the book entitled "Story of the Wreck of the Titanic" which was published in 1912 just after the Titanic had been struck by an iceberg and sank on her maiden voyage.

As the *Titanic* drew away from the wharf to begin her only voyage, a common emotion quickened the thousands who were aboard her. Grimy slaves who worked and withered deep down in the glaring heat of her boiler rooms, on her breezy decks men of achievement and fame and millionaire pleasure seekers for whom the boat provided
5   countless luxuries, in the steerage hordes of emigrants huddled in straited quarters but with their hearts fired for the new free land of hope; these, and also he whose anxious office placed him high above all — charged with the keeping of all their lives — this care-furrowed captain on the bridge, his many-varied passengers, and even the remotest menial of his crew, experienced alike a glow of triumph as they faced unknown
10   dangers of the deep, a triumph born of pride in the enormous, wonderful new ship that carried them.

For she was the biggest boat that ever had been in the world. She implied the utmost stretch of construction, the furthest achievement in efficiency, the bewildering embodiment of an immense multitude of luxuries for which only the richest of the earth could pay. The cost of the *Titanic* was tremendous — it had taken millions of dollars — many months to complete her. Besides (and best of all) she was practically unsinkable her owners said; pierce her hull anywhere, and behind was a watertight bulkhead, a sure defence to flout the floods and hold the angry ocean from its prey.

Angry is the word — for in all her triumph of perfection the *Titanic* was but man's latest insolence to the sea. Every article in her was a sheer defiance to the Deep's might and majesty. The ship is not the ocean's bride; steel hull and mast, whirling shaft and throbbing engine-heart (products, all, of serviceable wonderworking fire) — what kinship have these with the wild and watery waste? They are an affront and not an affinity for the cold and alien and elusive element that at all times threatens to overwhelm them.

But no one on the *Titanic* dreamed of danger when her prow was first set westward and her blades began the rhythmic beat that must not cease until the Atlantic had been crossed. Of all the statesmen, journalists, authors, famous financiers who were among her passengers (many of whom had arranged their affairs especially to secure passage in this splendid vessel), in all that brilliant company it may be doubted if a single mind secreted the faintest lurking premonition of a fear. Other ships could come safely and safely go, much more this monster — why, if an accident occurred and worse came to worst, she was literally too *big* to sink! Such was the instinctive reasoning of her passengers and crew, and such the unconsidered opinion of the world that read of her departure on the fatal day which marked the beginning of her first voyage and her last.

No doubt her very name tempted this opinion: *Titanic* was she titled — as though she were allied to the famous fabled giants of old called Titans, who waged a furious war with the very forces of creation.

Out she bore, this giant of the ships, then, blithely to meet and buffet back the surge, the shock, of ocean's elemental might; latest enginery devised in man's eternal warfare against nature, product of a thousand minds, bearer of myriad hopes. And to that unconsidered opinion of the world she doubtless seemed even arrogant in her plenitude of power, like the elements she clove and rode — the sweeping winds above, the surging tide below. But this would be only in daytime, when the *Titanic* was beheld near land, whereon are multitudes of things beside which the biggest of the ships loomed large. When we imagine her alone, eclipsed by the solitude and immensity of night, a gleaming speck — no more — upon the gulf and middle of the vasty deep, while her gayer guests are dancing and the rest are moved to mirth or wrapped in slumber or lulled in security — when we think of her thus in her true relation, she seems not arrogant of power at all; only a slim and alien shape too feeble for her freight of precious souls, plowing a tiny track across the void, set about with silent forces of destruction compared to which she is as fragile as a cockle shell.

Against her had been set in motion a mass for a long time mounting, a century's stored-up aggregation of force, greater than any man-made thing as is infinity to one. It had expanded in the patience of great solitudes. On a Greenland summit, ages ago, avalanches of ice and snow collided, welded and then moved, inches in a year, an evolution that had nought to do with time. It was the true inevitable, gouging-out a valley for its course, shouldering the precipices from its path. Finally the glacier reached the open Arctic, when a mile-in-width of it broke off and floated swinging free at last.

Does Providence directly govern everything that is? And did the Power who preordained the utmost second of each planet's journey, rouse up the mountain from its sleep of snow and send it down to drift, deliberately direct, into the exact moment in the sea of time, into the exact station in the sea of waters, where danced a gleaming speck — the tiny *Titanic* — to be touched and overborne?

It is easy thus to ascribe to the Infinite the direction of the spectacular phenomena of nature; our laws denote them "acts of God"; our instincts (after centuries of civilisation) still see in earthquakes an especial instance of His power, and in the flood of evidence of His wrath. The floating menace of the sea and ice is in a class with these. The terror-stricken who from their ship beheld the overwhelming monster say that it was beyond all imagination vast and awful, hundreds of feet high, leagues in extent, black as it moved beneath no moon, appallingly suggestive of man's futility amidst the immensity of creation. See how, by a mere touch — scarcely a jar — one of humanity's proudest handiworks, the greatest vessel of all time, is cut down in her course, ripped up, dismantled and engulfed. The true Titan has overturned the toy.

(Marshall Everett)

Model Paper A

Questions on the Passage

Marks

(a) Explain how the sentence structure and word choice in the first paragraph (lines 1–11) combine to create the emotions of those setting sail in the *Titanic*.   **4 A**

(b) In your own words explain in what ways the *Titanic* was assumed to be better than any previous ocean liner.   **4 U**

(c) Using your own words explain the feature of the *Titanic*'s structure which made people believe she was unsinkable.   **2 U**

(d) Explain how the imagery and word choice in lines 19–25 create an impression of the relationship between man and the sea.   **4 A/U**

(e) Look at ONE example of alliteration from paragraph 3 (lines 19–25), and explain whether you think it adds anything to the mood of the paragraph.   **2 E**

(f) Show how the context helps you to understand the meaning of "premonition" in line 31.   **2 U**

(g) Show how the sentence structure in lines 31–35 helps to emphasise the contrast between what we now know and what men thought at the time about the *Titanic*.   **4 A**

(h) Explain the significance of paragraph 5 (lines 36–38) to the passage as a whole.   **2 A**

(i) How do sound effects add to the mood at the start of *Titanic*'s journey in lines 39–44?   **4 A**

(j) How does the perspective, or way in which we look at the *Titanic*, change in paragraph 6 (lines 44–52)?   **2 U**

(k) "as fragile as a cockle shell" (line 52). How effective do you find this image of a great ship?   **2 E**

(l) In paragraph 7 (lines 53–59) the formation of the iceberg which struck the *Titanic* is described. Which aspects of the iceberg are emphasised?   **2 U**

Model Paper A

Marks

(m) Look carefully at lines 60–64. Show how the writer uses sentence structure and word choice to give his own moral view about what happened to the *Titanic*.

4 A

(n) Comment on the use of TWO of the following as they are used in the last paragraph:
    Inverted commas
    Brackets
    Dashes

2 A

(o) Examine the picture of the iceberg portrayed in the last paragraph. Think about the whole passage and then explain how effective you find the last sentence.

4 E/A

(p) The writer of this passage, in keeping with the mood of 1912, has taken a very moral look at the sinking of the *Titanic*.

By careful consideration of the passage as a whole, explain how the writer manages to suggest even from the beginning that Man will be punished for thinking that he could build an "unsinkable" ship.

6 A/U

(q) Look again at paragraph 1 (lines 1–11) and at the last paragraph (lines 65–74).

Compare these two paragraphs.
To what extent would you say that the writer has effectively shown a change of mood from the start of the journey to the ship's final destruction?

You must refer to tone, imagery, structure, etc.

10 E/A

Total = (60)

A = 32

U = 17

E = 11

Model Paper A

ANSWERS

Marks

(a) **Explain how the sentence structure and word choice in the first paragraph (lines 1–11) combine to create the emotions of those setting sail in the *Titanic*.**

4 A

EXCITEMENT — ANTICIPATION — PRIDE

Opening sentence sets the subject. It is comparatively short compared with the long sentence to follow.
Then a series of NOUN phrases without main verbs indicating different types of people on board.
This is picked up after the semi-colon by "these" giving a sense of dramatic numbers. "and he" introduces a new figure, but there are two more phrases, one in parenthesis indicated by dashes, before we learn who it is.
Build up to a climax of phrases with repetition of "triumph".

Marks: points made simply 1 mark each. Developed analysis of a point would get 2 points.

(b) **In your own words explain in what ways the *Titanic* was assumed to be better than any previous ocean liner.**

4 U

"biggest". She was larger.
"stretch of construction". She had been more skilfully built.
"efficiency". She would work more effectively.
"multitude of luxuries". She had more excessive delights for the very rich.

Marks: 1 each but own words must be used.

(c) **Using your own words explain the feature of the *Titanic's* structure which made people believe she was unsinkable.**

2 U

Even if something went through her bodywork there was a a defensive layer beneath which would stop the water getting into the whole ship.

(d) **Explain how the imagery and word choice in lines 18–25 create an impression of the relationship between man and the sea.**

4 A/U

INCOMPATIBLE — SEA IS SUPERIOR — MAN INFERIOR — MAN INSOLENT TO THE SEA

Sea — "angry" suggests indignation at man. "might and majesty" suggests it is worthy of respect. "wild and watery" suggests the sea is alien and dangerous.

Man — "flout", "sheer defiance", suggests man is cheeky and rude in defying the sea, "insolence" repeats and sums up this idea.

"not the . . . bride" suggests man thinks he is linked but mistaken.

List of mechanical features suggest how puny man made efforts are as he defies the sea.

"wonderworking fire" suggests even the strength of man's efforts is not likely to affect the sea, literally fire and water are incompatible.

Marks: relationship must be discussed for full marks. 2 marks for each linked idea.

(e) **Look at ONE example of alliteration from paragraph 3 (lines 19–25), and explain whether you think it adds anything to the mood of the paragraph.**   2 E

Plenty of choice. They could show dramatic importance or some of them could be clichés.

defiance of the Deep
might and majesty
wild and watery waste

Marks: 1 for picking out an example. 1 for a proper reason as to why it does or does not add to the mood.

(f) **Show how the context helps you to understand the meaning of "premonition" in line 31.**   2 U

Means an advance mental warning of what was to come.

Context looks to the future. Then shows the confidence of the passengers and their refusal to fear. "fatal day" tells us that they should be taking warning.

Marks: 1 for definition; 1 for linking it to the context.

(g) **Show how the sentence structure in lines 31–35 helps to emphasise the contrast between what we now know and what men thought at the time about the *Titanic*.**   4 A

Confident opening then a dash. Colloquial "why if" and exclamation indicating their scorn at the idea of disaster .
Repeated pattern of "Such was" to emphasise the confidence of everyone in the ship.

Simpler ending to the sentence "that read of her departure . . ." Use of "and" in "her first voyage and her last".

Marks: 2 marks for each comment fully explained.

(h) **Explain the significance of paragraph 5 (lines 36–38) to the passage as a whole.**   2 A

Background idea. It explains the name, and this image of the ancient giants will recur in the passage.

Marks: 1 for background, 1 for reference to later use of the image.

(i) **How do sound effects add to the mood at the start of *Titanic's* journey in lines 39–44?**   4 A

EXCITEMENT — CONFIDENCE

Sounds, onomatopoeia, like "buffet", "surge", "shock", suggest force and anger of the sea.
Internal assonance of "clove and rode" suggest continuous movement.
Alliteration and long vowels of "sweeping . . . surging" suggest magnificence and confidence.

Marks: Sounds must be linked to mood. Example and explanation = 2.

(j) **How does the perspective, or way in which we look at the *Titanic*, change in paragraph 6 (lines 44–52)?** 2 U

We have looked closely at the *Titanic* near land and it seemed large.
We then look at it from a distance against the vastness of the sea and it seems tiny, "slim", "feeble", "fragile".

Marks: change in perspective needed for 2 marks.

(k) **"as fragile as a cockle shell" (line 52). How effective do you find this image of a great ship?** 2 E

Effective if we think of a great ship against the huge ocean.
Not so good if we think of shape and nature of a cockle shell.
Own judgment needed but must include an explanation.

Marks: 2 for the analysis and explanation. BUT no marks if no evaluation made.

(l) **In paragraph 7 (lines 53–59) the formation of the iceberg which struck the *Titanic* is described. Which aspects of the iceberg are emphasised?** 2 U

Force
Size
Age
Determination

Marks: Half a mark for each point made.

(m) **Look carefully at lines 60–64. Show how the writer uses sentence structure and word choice to give his own moral view about what happened to the *Titanic*.** 4 A

Rhetorical questions suggests that the answer is yes, Providence does govern all.
Sentence beginning with "And" suggests one idea flows from the last.
Repeated pattern of "into the exact" stresses the inevitability of the destruction.
Dashes to separate the phrase "tiny *Titanic*" emphasising how small it is compared to the forces against it.

Words such as "Providence", "Power" and "preordained" suggest a greater power than man at work.
Words like "sleep" personify the iceberg and give it a sense of a giant aroused by man's stupidity,
"exact" gives a sense of purpose and intention to the iceberg.

Marks: Both sentence structure and word choice must be looked at.
       2 marks each for well developed points.

Model Paper A

(n) **Comment on the use of TWO of the following as they are used in the last paragraph:**
    Inverted commas
    Brackets
    Dashes

2 A

Inverted commas = quotation.
Brackets = a piece of information added, in this case almost sarcastically, to suggest that civilisation has not cured us of our instinctive beliefs.
Dashes = parenthesis, like brackets, adding a piece of further information, in this case repeating the idea of the tiny blow that was needed.

Marks: 1 each.

(o) **Examine the picture of the iceberg portrayed in the last paragraph. Think about the whole passage and then explain how effective you find the last sentence.**

4 E/A

Great size and terrifying quality emphasised and the ship is seen as easily overthrown by its force.
The passage as a whole has emphasised man's folly in thinking he could defeat the power of Nature.
The image of the real Titans, who were powerful gods of old, has already been touched on.

The last sentence therefore contains all these ideas, i.e., of size and godlike qualities.
The ship is now spoken of as a "toy", emphasising its childish imitation of greater things.

Marks: 2 for looking at the rest of the passage; 2 for weighing up the effectiveness of the last sentence.

(p) **The writer of this passage, in keeping with the mood of 1912, has taken a very moral look at the sinking of the *Titanic*.**

By careful consideration of the passage as a whole, explain how the writer manages to suggest even from the beginning that Man will be punished for thinking that he could build an "unsinkable" ship.

6 U/A

This requires a look at general points made throughout the passage.
First paragraph suggests over-confidence and pride + quote.
Second suggests over-confidence against attack + quote.
Third suggests that the sea is angry and powerful + quote.
Fourth again suggests over-confidence + quote.
Sixth suggests how really tiny the ship is + quote.
Seventh suggests Providence is preparing a punishment + quote.
Last two continue the idea of Providence or God taking a hand and directing the punishment for man's insolence + quote.

Marks: at least three **different** points should be made and supported by references to the text. E.g., man's pride, man's insolence, greater power of the sea.

Model Paper A

(q) **Look again at paragraph 1 (lines 1–11) and at the last paragraph (lines 65–74).**

Compare these two paragraphs.
To what extent would you say that the writer has effectively shown a change of mood from the start of the journey to the ship's final destruction?

You must refer to tone, imagery, structure, etc.   10   E/A

Use information and ideas already discussed but make sure that a comparison is made.

1st Paragraph	*Last Paragraph*
Pride	Terror
Great size of ship	Smallness of ship
Individual types mentioned	General — the terror-stricken
Warmth of emotion "fired" "hope"	Violence "ripped" engulfed"
Superiority "high above"	Insignificance "toy"
Cheerful "breezy decks"	Awesome "vast and awful"

Some similarities

Common emotion	The terror-stricken
Melodramatic — unknown dangers	cut down
Sentences build to a climax in each	
Excess but of luxury	Excess of size of monster iceberg

Marks: many other points could be made and made differently. A good full answer for full marks. References to the text and to features of style must be made.

Total =   (60)

A = 32

U = 17

E = 11

MODEL PAPER B

HIGHER ENGLISH **Interpretation** **NATIONAL QUALIFICATIONS**

Time: 1 hour 30 minutes

You should attempt all questions.

The total value of the Paper is 60 marks.

INTERPRETATION

There is ONE passage and questions.

Read the passage carefully and then answer all the questions which follow. **Use your own words whenever possible and particularly when you are instructed to do so.**

You should read the passage to:

- understand what the author has to say about the journey in the past to Petra, and what he observed when he visited it in recent times (**Understanding — U**);

- analyse the choice of language, imagery and structures to show how they convey his point of view and contribute to the impact of what he saw (**Analysis — A**);

- evaluate how effectively he has achieved his purpose (**Evaluation — E**).

A code letter (U, A, E) is used alongside each question to give some indication of the skills being assessed. The number of marks attached to each question will give some indication of the length and kind of answer required.

Don Belt, writing in the "National Geographic" describes the city of Petra in Jordan, as it was in the past and as it is now.

It took 12 weeks to get here from the frankincense groves of Oman, once the camels were loaded and the campfires stamped out. Then the caravan, single-minded as a line of ants, would set out through the morning mist, guarding its precious cargo from bandits, and pass uneasily, single file, through the treachery of Yemen.

5   Later, if things were going well, the caravan would pause to trade at Medina, drinking from its brackish wells, and gathering strength for the journey ahead. Then it would strike out north across the hellish, flint-strewn sands of western Arabia, living from one water hole to the next all the way to the capital of the Nabataeans, who ruled the lands east of the Jordan River. To the camel driver of two millennia ago, this city, Petra,
10   beckoned like a distant star.

What a relief it must have been to see the guards on red sandstone ledges, and to be waved in after paying the toll, and to breathe the cool air inside the Siq (pronounced seek), the 250-foot-high crack in the rock that was, and still is, the main road into Petra.

For the thirsty there was water, lots of it, flowing down sinuous stone channels along the roadway; for the grateful and devout there were carved altars to Dushara, the head Nabataean god, on the chasm's sandstone walls. Boys on donkeys would dash by, shouting news of the arrival; the smell of cardamom, campfires, and searing meat promised hospitality just ahead. Finally, the caravan would swing wide around a bend to face Al Khazneh (the Treasury), that towering edifice carved from rose-coloured rock, and plunge into the crowded marketplace beyond.

Two thousand years have passed, but shades of ancient Petra still endure in the desert of southern Jordan. The facades of its buildings peer out from banks of drifted sand, and you can wander freely among them, fingertips on chiselled rock. Delicate bits of Nabataean pottery lie scattered across the land like eggshells, so numerous at times that it's hard to avoid stepping on them. And if you're out early — before the first tourist bus pulls up just past daybreak — you might even hear echoes of the ancient city, as I have, in the local Bedouin drifting by on camels in the mist or in the murmur of voices over pots of steeping tea.

After dozens of visits I've come to recognise this immediacy of the past as Petra's surpassing charm. Yet it's also the site's most profound dilemma: A living antiquity presents problems to those who would preserve the past, or uncover its secrets, or package it for mass consumption.

Like other nomadic peoples who wandered through the spotlight of history, the Nabataeans left little behind to explain themselves. They probably moved into Palestine from Arabia several centuries before Christ. By the first century B.C. their capital was a rich city shaped by the sophistication and wealth that Petra, a natural fortress on a pass through rugged mountains, acquired as a crossroads for trade.

Filling a power vacuum left by Greece's decline, the Nabataeans dominated this part of the Middle East for more than four centuries before being subjugated by the Romans, then eclipsed by the Byzantines, and finally dispersed onto the back lot of history. From sherds of their pottery we know they were artists: ancient manuscripts describe them as shrewd traders and merchants. Both qualities are reflected in Petra's public architecture, a dizzying array of temples, tombs, theatres, and other buildings chiselled out of russet sandstone. Scattered over 400 square miles and connected by trails and caravan roads, these buildings are monumental and dramatic even when judged against the Greek masterpieces of the day.

But their breakthrough achievement — the one that made all the others possible — came when the Nabataeans mastered their water supply, which enabled them to build a metropolis of 30,000 in a remote desert canyon that gets only six inches of rain each year.

Harvesting water like precious grain, the Nabataeans collected it, piped it, stored it, conserved it, prayed over it, managed it — by devising elaborate systems of hydraulics that make up, even now, the unseen musculature of Petra. Hundreds of cisterns kept Petra from dying of thirst in times of drought, while masonry dams in the surrounding hills protected the city from flash floods after bursts of rain.

That kind of planning is called for again today — as Jordan, for whom Petra is supreme in a collection of archaeological treasures, weighs decisions about how best to excavate and preserve the site while reaping economic benefit from the world's growing interest in it.

With no oil fields and few natural resources, Jordan greets the thousands of tourists who come pouring down the Siq into Petra as joyously as rainfall in the desert. The challenge will be to keep this flood of visitors from sweeping away the very features that make the place unique.

I first met Hamoudi al-Bedouin in a Nabataean tomb, and even there he made quite an impression. It was shortly after dawn in a stone chamber twelve feet square and six feet under, illuminated only by the murky plume of daylight that filled the rock chimney we'd used to get in.

We were excavating beneath the ruins of a fifth-century A.D. Byzantine church in Petra, and the dust was already thick enough to muffle the growl of Hamoudi's shovel as he carved chunks of hardpacked sand from a nearby grave, then deposited them gently onto the screen of my wooden sifter. I would shake the sand through, as if panning for gold, and Hamoudi would pause to check the debris left behind, plucking out sherds of pottery with fingers as fluent and precise as the bill of a bird.

With so much of Petra still underground, practically every stab of a shovel yields something worth talking about. There were nearly two dozen archaeological projects under way the last time I was there, ranging from a study measuring the effect of wind erosion on Petra's sandstone facades to the unearthing of a massive building along the main street.

Some of the most spectacular recent finds involve the Siq, the cliff-lined road into Petra that was buried under sand and flood debris. In the mountains overlooking it, engineers have begun to retrace and map the Nabataeans' network of channels, basins and dams — all built to capture and control spring water and the rainfall that gushes down towards the Siq through 19 distinct tributaries.

"We were astonished by how sophisticated their ideas were," said Maan al-Huneidi, who manages the project, the day I scrambled for hours over waterworks with one of his lead engineers. We found dozens of sand-filled dams tucked into the mountainside that day and almost as many cisterns carved from solid rock. Miniature canals linked one catchment area to the next, moving water downhill gracefully, sometimes whimsically, in little troughs of sandstone as finely carved as sculpture.

Last year Maan's company removed some 400,000 cubic feet of rubble from the Siq's floor, exposing the original pavement and ancient features on the chasm walls, including ceramic water pipes and a giant camel caravan carved in bas-relief from the sandstone.

I watched one morning as dozens of tourists admired this monumental carving, which is just above eye level. Some ran their hands over the stone, bringing down a faint shower of sand, while others picked idly at the wall for souvenirs. At one point a tour guide mounted a nearby Nabataean channel to deliver his spiel; he failed to mention that the plaster crumbling under his feet was two millennia old.

That man was lucky that Aysar Akrawi didn't catch his act the morning she and I toured the Siq together. As director of the nongovernmental Petra National Trust, Akwari helped raise the half million dollars it cost to excavate the Siq — only to be reminded, daily, of how vulnerable it is once exposed.

"Petra is an exceptionally fragile site," she said moments after a little boy blissfully urinated in front of us on the sandstone steps of the Treasury, Petra's most famous building. "To overdevelop it for tourism without protecting these antiques is a huge mistake."

There is a quiet grandeur to Petra that eludes the casual tourist, many of whom trek down the Siq to the Treasury and back out again without pausing longer than the time it takes to buy a bottle of water and a "Petra, Jordan" T-shirt. This is exactly what I did the first time I visited, giving the place a few hours one spring afternoon, seeing only a fraction of the hundred square miles that Jordan set aside as a national park in 1993.

From its centre Petra extends for miles in all directions along a network of wadis, or dry riverbeds, and old caravan roads that once moved frankincense from Oman to Gaza and bracelets of gold from workshops in Aleppo to the suqs of Yemen. In recent years I've retraced those routes and felt the presence of the ancient world in everything from the plaintive travelling songs of the Bedouin to the sandpaper swish of a camel's hoof on sandstone, each big as a salad plate, soft as a paw.

Time pokes along haphazardly here, moving to the ever changing rhythms of sun and grass and goats. One afternoon Hamoudi and I dropped by the men's tent at a wedding feast near Beida, a tree-lined wadi that serves as Petra's back door. Hamoudi, who is at home anywhere, folded his lank frame gracefully onto shaded mattresses after greeting the groom's father with fervent kisses on both cheeks. Hamoudi didn't know this family — they were of a different tribe — but for all anyone knew, he might have been a long-lost brother.

In the Petra backcountry you still find some of Hamoudi's tribe, called the Bedoul, dwelling in caves, as they have for centuries. For me, this human dimension is what breathes life into Petra and elevates the place from scenic to sublime — although I understand why most of the Bedoul, including Hamoudi and his family, live today in government houses in Umm Sayhun, a dreary little village of about 1,500 overlooking the land they once called their own.

After Petra was made a UNESCO world heritage site in 1985, the tribe moved out of the caves at the government's request and with an understanding that they'd continue working inside Petra as archaeologists, labourers, and vendors while grazing their goats in the countryside. In Umm Sayhun the Bedoul have access to schools, electricity, and health care — services that have enhanced their lives.

Yet if it weren't for his four children, Hamoudi, Bedouin to the core, would prefer to sleep in the open every night. In fact, many of the villagers vanish into the countryside at the first sign of warm weather, and those who stay behind usually camp out too — on the roofs of their government houses. And though squeezed into a village, the Bedoul still know this vast region better than anyone else. When a tourist wanders off in the desert and winds up dehydrated, it's not the army, which guards Petra, that finds him, revives him, and brings him in on the back of a camel or in the bed of a pickup truck. It's one of the Bedoul.

(Don Belt)

Model Paper B

Questions on the Passage

Marks

(a) By careful reference to word choice and imagery, explain the moods created by the first paragraph, lines 1–4.

4 U/A

(b) Look carefully at paragraph 2, lines 5–10. How does the language contribute to the sense of purpose?

3 A

(c) How does the sentence structure contribute to the atmosphere of paragraph 4, lines 14–20?

4 A

(d) "Two thousand years have passed" (line 21). How does this phrase contribute to the structure of the whole article?

2 A

(e) What is the dilemma (line 30) facing those interested in Petra today?

2 U

(f) How does the context help you to arrive at the meaning of "power vacuum" in line 38?

2 U

(g) Look carefully at the images in lines 51–55. Do you think they are appropriate for the description of gathering water?

4 A/E

(h) Look again at lines 33–50. Summarise briefly the history of Petra, using your own words.

6 U

(i) Look at lines 60–63. How does the imagery emphasise the problem faced by Jordan over Petra?

4 A/U

(j) What is the purpose of paragraph 14 (lines 64–67) in the overall structure of the passage.

2 A

(k) Look at the description of Hamoudi checking the debris in lines 72–73. How does the imagery contribute to our impression of his character?

3 A/U

(l) Look at lines 51–55 and lines 84–89. Explain how the ancient people of Petra managed to control their water supply.

6 U

(m) Comment on the irony in lines 94–98. 2 U

(n) Choose one of the images used to describe the camel (lines 117–118). Explain how effective you find it. 2 A/E

(o) What is the impression of the passing of Time created by the image "Time pokes along haphazardly here" in line 119? 2 A

(p) How effective do you find the last two sentences (lines 141–144) as an ending for the passage? 4 A/E

(q) Look again at lines 11–20 in the first half of the passage describing 2000 years ago.

Look again at lines 126–136 in the second half of the passage describing modern times.

How effectively does the writer bring out the change in atmosphere from past to present times?
You should consider: sentence structure, word choice, imagery, etc. 8 A/E

Total = (60)

A = $27\frac{1}{2}$

U = $23\frac{1}{2}$

E = 9

Model Paper B

ANSWERS *Marks*

(a) **By careful reference to word choice and imagery, explain the moods created by the first paragraph, lines 1–4.**   4 U/A

TWO moods at least should be identified.
DETERMINED   is suggested by forceful verbs "stamped out" and "set out".
and by image of the "ants" who are described as single minded and are known for their relentless movement.

UNEASY / NERVOUS is suggested by actual word "uneasily" and "guarding" as though they know there is danger. "bandits" and "treachery" suggest enemies about. "line of ants" suggests they are tiny and vulnerable.

Marks: 2 for understanding moods.
2 for analysing the language feature.

(b) **Look carefully at paragraph 2, lines 5–10. How does the language contribute to the sense of purpose?**   3 A

Vocabulary / word choice of "gathering strength" and "strike out" suggest force of their intentions almost like a fighter preparing for battle.
Image of living "from one water hole to the next" suggests keeping going at a very basic level of survival.
Image (metaphor) of their goal, "Petra beckoned like a distant star", suggests almost divine guidance as though they cannot escape their purpose.

Marks: $1^1/_2$ for each suitable word / phrase selected and analysed.

(c) **How does the sentence structure contribute to the atmosphere of paragraph 4, lines 14–20?**   4 A

Atmosphere must be stated — CONTENTED, HAPPY, RELIEVED, SATISFACTORY.
Repetition of "For the . . ." divided by semi-colon.
Good things mentioned then described by a series of phrases —
"Water, lots . . ."
"Altars to Dushara, the head . . ."

Items listed — "the smell of . . ."
The semi-colon in second sentence giving one noisy event, then followed by the list above.
The adverb "Finally," starting a sentence and then the long delay as the clause describes the bend round the treasury leading to the dramatic "and then plunge".

Marks: Atmosphere must be mentioned and two comments made on sentence structure for full marks.

(d) **"Two thousand years have passed" (line 21). How does this phrase contribute to the structure of the whole article?** 2 A

A turning point.
The passage has been describing the **past** arrivals at Petra; now it moves on to the **present**.

Marks: 1 only for just saying a turning point. Explanation needed for full marks.

(e) **What is the dilemma (line 30) facing those interested in Petra today?** 2 U

A dilemma is a problem where there are two alternatives, each dependent on the other, and it is difficult to choose either one without doing something wrong.

In this case it is good to find out Petra's secret history and to encourage tourists BUT by doing so it makes it hard to preserve Petra exactly as it was in the past.

Marks: 1 for each alternative.

(f) **How does the context help you to arrive at the meaning of "power vacuum" in line 38?** 2 U

A power vacuum is a gap in the government of an area which must be filled because it is needed.

Loss of power in Greece suggests something being removed, Filling suggests something moving in to a gap left. "the Nabataeans dominated" suggests an important or powerful nation taking over.

Marks: Definition = 1 then a satisfactory explanation making at least two of the points above for 1 mark.

(g) **Look carefully at the images in lines 51–55. Do you think they are appropriate for the description of gathering water?** 4 A/E

Simile — "like precious grain" emphasises the idea of harvesting as though it were equal to bread of life.
Image of Petra as a body needing nourishment is emphasised by the words like "musculature" to emphasise the idea of water being pumped round. "dying of thirst" keeps up the idea of human life needing the water

Marks: Images must be selected but in each case the answer must weigh up the suitability of the image to describe water being pumped round a city.

(h) **Look again at lines 33–50. Summarise briefly the history of Petra, using your own words.**   6 U

Main points should be made only and **using own words** will indicate an understanding of the vocabulary.
Came from Arabia to Palestine long before time of Christ.
By 1st century BC they dominated militarily and in trade.
After 400 years they were overrun by the Romans.
Then the Byzantine Empire took over the area.
Petra was forgotten as a world power.
Their greatest achievement was the provision of water supplies in an area of 6 inches of rain annually.

Marks: No marks for just quoting. Points do not have to be made exactly as above but they should be made briefly.

(i) **Look at lines 60–63. How does the imagery emphasise the problem faced by Jordan over Petra?**   4 A/U

Jordan needs tourists to earn money so image of "rainfall" appropriate in this desert area. Rain can be harmful if it becomes a "flood" so that is appropriate if the visitors destroy Petra by coming in too great numbers.

Marks: 2 for each aspect of the image. (Acceptable to link the image to idea of Petra's past control of the water supply).

(j) **What is the purpose of paragraph 14 (lines 64–67) in the overall structure of the passage.**   2 A

Another turning point. The writer is moving on to the people working in Petra either as archaeologists or as tour guides.

Marks: 1 for turning point but explanation needed for full marks.

(k) **Look at the description of Hamoudi checking the debris in lines 72–73. How does the imagery contribute to our impression of his character?**   3 A/U

A CAREFUL, METICULOUS MAN.
Image of a small bird pecking tiny amounts of grain stresses how carefully and precisely he is checking the the tiny grains of sand and pottery.

Marks: 1 for his character. 2 for an analysis of the image.

(l) **Look at lines 51–55 and lines 84–89. Explain how the ancient people of Petra managed to control their water supply.**   6 U

Water was collected in great containers (cisterns).
It was pumped round the city (hydraulics).
Dams held the water back in the hill rivers so that it did not just rush down on the city.

A series of dams and basins controlled the flow of the water from the small rivers.
Small canals linked the different containers.
The water flowed gently downhill through them.

Marks: Clear points should be made and where possible own words used.

Model Paper B

(m) **Comment on the irony in lines 94–98.** 2 U

The tour guide depends on the remains for his career yet he is destroying them by standing on them.

OR The tour guide is supposed to know about the ancient history yet he does not seem to realise how old the stone channel is that he is standing on.

Marks: either of these explanations is acceptable.

(n) **Choose one of the images used to describe the camel (lines 117–118). Explain how effective you find it.** 2 A/E

"Sandpaper swish"	Sound
"big as a salad plate"	Size
"soft as a paw'"	Feel

Marks: 2 for analysis and explanation of how effective it is.

(o) **What is the impression of the passing of Time created by the image "Time pokes along haphazardly here" in line 119?** 2 A

PASSING SLOWLY
"pokes along" suggests goes in fits and starts, moves forward very slowly. "haphazard" adds the idea of lack of purpose now.

Marks: 1 for the impression; 1 for the explanation.

(p) **How effective do you find the last two sentences (lines 141–144) as an ending for the passage?** 4 A/E

Meaning: Passage has talked of past and present emphasising the strengths of the past. This reinforces the idea, gives an example of a skill that has survived.

Style: Long sentence including the Negative "it's not . . ." leading up to short, dramatic final sentence.

Marks: 2 for a reasonable suggestion. The answer must comment on the passage as a whole.

Model Paper B

(q) **Look again at lines 11–20 in the first half of the passage describing 2000 years ago.**

Look again at lines 126–136 in the second half of the passage describing modern times.

How effectively does the writer bring out the change in atmosphere from past to present times?
You should consider: sentence structure, word choice, imagery, etc. 8 A/E

This requires comparison.
Extract 1 is contented, civilised, busy, romantic, magnificent.
Extract 2 is down-to-earth, efficient, dull, etc.

Marks: not necessarily 4 each but a reasonably balanced answer needed.

Total = (60)

A = $27\frac{1}{2}$

U = $23\frac{1}{2}$

E = 9

| HIGHER ENGLISH | **MODEL PAPER C**
Interpretation | NATIONAL QUALIFICATIONS |

Time: 1 hour 30 minutes

You should attempt all questions.

The total value of the Paper is 60 marks.

INTERPRETATION

There are TWO passages and questions.

Read the passages carefully and then answer all the questions which follow. **Use your own words whenever possible and particularly when you are instructed to do so.**

You should read the passages to:

- understand what the writers have to say about the problems of those manning lighthouses (**Understanding — U**);

- analyse the choice of language, imagery and structures to show how they convey the point of view (**Analysis — A**);

- evaluate how effectively each writer has achieved his purpose (**Evaluation — E**).

A code letter (U, A, E) is used alongside each question to give some indication of the skills being assessed. The number of marks attached to each question will give some indication of the length and kind of answer required.

PASSAGE 1

The first passage is taken from "A History of Lighthouses" by Patrick Beaver; the second passage is taken from an interview held with a man, Keeper Christie, who had been a lighthouse keeper for many years. It appears in the book "Lighthouses and Lightships" by Lee Chadwick.

The Light-keeper's World

Innumerable tales of romance, of blood and of thunder in particular have been written about the men — and women — whose task it has been to keep the lights in sea-swept towers. These stories were especially popular in Victorian times and from them it would appear that, far from being a life of boredom and isolation, the light-keeper's lot seldom
5 contained a dull moment. Murder, mayhem, suicide and sudden insanity would appear to have been commonplace on isolated rock stations — more than one keeper having been rumoured, for one reason or another, as having turned whitehaired overnight. Many a little child, its parents having been murdered or kidnapped by wreckers, was, we are asked to believe, left alone to tend the light and (to judge by the illustrations)
10 compelled to stand on the family Bible in order to reach the lantern. But sensational and fantastic as these stories may be, they contain a basis of truth, for any job that entails constant exposure to the forces of nature must have its dramas and its dangers, and when the job also involves long periods of isolation the dangers and dramas will be multiplied.

A tragi-comic incident occurred in 1928 on an isolated cay in the Bahamas which was then guarded by a beacon known as Double-headed Shot light. The keeper, who lived on the cay with his family, died suddenly. No relief was expected for several days and, because of the warm climate, the family were faced with the task of burying the body without delay. No grave could be dug as the islet is composed of hard rock, and the only suitable spot for interment was a natural hole in the rock. Into this the body was lowered in a standing-up position, a stone being placed over the top. During the makeshift ceremony a violent storm blew up and as the family made their way from the improvised tomb to the lighthouse they heard a loud report which made them turn their heads towards the grave, just in time to see the corpse shoot, head first, into the air like a rocket. The cavity chosen as the keeper's tomb was a blow hole!

It is not surprising that friction existed among men confined together in isolated or wave-swept stations, in particular where keepers were unable to put more than a few yards between themselves. In such stations as Eddystone, Rothersand or Minot's Ledge, for instance, the only retreat from the rooms of the tower is the outside gallery which, windy and confined, is hardly the best place for a walk.

Smeaton relates that while on a visit to Eddystone he learned that the two keepers there had not spoken to each other for a month, and goes on to remark that candidates for the position of light-keeper must be naturally morose and perhaps slightly misanthropic!

The Literature for Lighthouses Mission supplied small libraries which were changed with each relief and which consisted of "... a Bible and Prayer book and books suitable for persons of their class". Fishing, of course, has always been popular among keepers, and where it is not possible to cast a line clear of the rocks, kite-fishing is resorted to. It was, perhaps, an attempt to catch fish which led to a mystery that will always remain a classic of the sea and of lighthouses in particular.

Standing twenty-two miles off the Isle of Lewis among the Hebridean Islands is a cluster of isolated rocks known as the Seven Hunters, or the Flannan Islands, on one of the highest of which stands a tower erected by David and Charles Stevenson. It is so desolate a spot in winter, frequented by so little shipping, that the light may flash heedlessly for nights on end. On Boxing Day, 1900, the relief tender made its fortnightly visit to the Flannan light but the crew were surprised that, on approaching, the usual signals were absent; so was the appearance of the keepers who invariably came down to the landing stage to greet them. Now thoroughly puzzled, the crew of the tender made their way inside the lighthouse and found it completely deserted, while a search made of the rocks yielded no trace of the missing keepers. An examination of the log showed the last entry as having been at 4 a.m. nearly a week previously; the lamp had not been abandoned but had burned out of oil. Many sensational rumours were circulated and even published purporting to explain the mystery, including the favourite lighthouse story of sudden insanity and murder, but there was not the slightest sign on the rock or in the tower that could explain the sudden disappearance of three men. It must be assumed that one of them went out onto the rock and was swept into the sea by the violent storm that was then blowing. His companions in attempting to rescue him were also caught by the sea and swept in after him.

Even though most isolated light-stations are now equipped with television sets, the modern keeper spends most of his leisure time in much the same way as did his predecessors. In fact he probably spends less time gazing at the television screen than does the average landlubber. Much of his time is spent in such occupations as model-making and painting; in addition the isolated lighthouse makes an ideal place for study. Lighthouse authorities receive a steady flow of applications from students who want to spend a limited time as a lighthouse keeper in order to prepare for an examination. These requests, of course, cannot be granted.

The conditions of entry and service as a keeper to Trinity House lighthouse service are fairly typical. Applicants must be between eighteen and thirty-two years of age and the first listed requirement is that they must be dentally fit — a very wise rule, one would agree, at the thought of being marooned on Eddystone with a raging toothache. On appointment the recruit spends four weeks at Harwich taking instruction in the various types of equipment: explosive fog signals; Morse and semaphore signalling; cookery, first aid; radio telephony, etc. He then goes to a shore lighthouse where he receives further instruction in the handling of equipment. It is likely that his first permanent station will be one of the old isolated towers, it being a logical deduction that if a man can prove himself satisfactory and can himself stand life in the confined and monotonous surroundings of a sea-swept tower such as Wolf Rock, that if he does not allow his companions to get on his nerves and does not himself get on theirs, then he should be perfectly happy in the service when his turn comes to be posted ashore. In practice only about half the entrants stay the course of the first year — the others return to more prosaic occupations.

A few years ago one Edward Wood went to Bishop's Rock to make a Christmas Day broadcast for the BBC. While he was there he marvelled at the "cheerfulness and philosophic calm" with which the keepers carried out their duties. Mr Wood had intended his visit to Bishop's Rock to last three days, but during his stay the weather turned nasty. Four weeks later he managed to get ashore.

(Patrick Beaver)

PASSAGE 2

In the late autumn of 1968 I arrived on the Lighthouse Hills of Cromer in torrential rain. It was one of those East Anglian days when the grey line of the North Sea merges with the immense dome of the sky. I looked down at the sands and the white edge of foam far below where some say the vanished village of Shipden lies, long ago swallowed up by the
5   devouring sea. Wind tore at the silver sea buckthorn and the dark heather, and that day the Lighthouse Hills took on some of the wildness that made them the legendary home of Black Shuck — the ghost hound brought over by the Vikings and said to haunt this part of England ever since.

    Nothing, however, could be more solid and reassuring than Cromer Lighthouse. The
10 two strongly built keeper's cottages at the foot of the fine tower had been recently modernised and I noticed the excellent condition of the paintwork as I rang the bell of one of them.

    Soon the door was opened by Keeper Christie himself, looking much too young to be about to retire. In fact, he measured up in every way to the story book descriptions of
15 lighthouse keepers, even to "the eyes grown blue with long looking at the sea!'

    We talked in a pleasant living room from where, through an open door, could be seen a modern kitchen. The cheerful blaze of the fire seemed extra cosy in contrast to the rain clouds scudding past outside and Keeper Christie, his dog beside him, wasted no time in answering my questions. I admired his accommodation.

20 "Each keeper's dwelling," he said, "has a kitchen and scullery with a gas stove, a sitting room, three bedrooms and a bathroom. There are hot radiators in the sitting room. What a difference from the old days of black coal stoves, no hot water, tin bath and water pumped from the well after being collected from the roof."

    I was interested in the manning of the station and the division of duties. He explained
25 that normally there are three keepers to a shore station but Cromer is "two handed". This is because there is no fog signal here. A local man comes for two days a week to give each keeper an off-duty day. Two men must be on the station after dark, whether or not on duty, so the only time it is possible to leave the station after dark is on off-duty day.

30 Watch keeping arrangements are decided by the District Superintendent concerned and of course vary according to the station and the state of the weather. What, I asked, would be a typical week's work in a lighthouse? "The main duty," replied Mr Christie, "is of course as in all lighthouses, the care of the light, to ensure that it always gives the correct flashing pattern. A check must also be made that the standby equipment is in
35 perfect order so that it is ready in case of breakdown. The Radio beacon is timed to the second and is as important as the light.

    "Even in these days of wireless weather reports, someone has to be in hearing of the telephone at all times because Cromer is a gale warning station and a message may come through at any moment to hoist the cone as a warning to shipping." (I had in fact
40 noticed on arrival that the cone was aloft, hoisted point upwards to indicate a northerly gale.)

    When it came to answering questions on his own personal adventures in the service, Mr Christie was much more reticent. With a smile, he quietly replied: "I am one of those people to whom nothing ever happens."

One of the first things I noticed on the walls of the sitting room were two paintings of lighthouses. These I learnt were his own work. Both were of rock stations painted in his leisure hours during his service at the Smalls and the South Bishop Rock off the Pembrokeshire coast of Wales. As Mr Christie pointed out:

"The virtue of painting as a rock station hobby is that it is a silent one. When others are sleeping, a noisy hobby like wood-work in an echoing tower can make you rather unpopular."

Then at last we talked of his personal memories — how he had served for an unusually long time at a stretch (twenty-eight years) without being appointed to a land station.

"I thoroughly enjoy the peace and quiet of the life but in time everyone needs a break from rock stations because of the strain of living in such a confined space. At the Smalls, for instance, it was literally impossible to go out. At times, massive shattering waves swept the rocks and the only creatures who could safely bask there were seals. There was the case of two men washed overboard about forty years ago, one at the Longships and one at the Wolf Rock. At the Wolf the drowning man was seen pulling off his seaboots to lighten himself but the tide was too strong and he was dragged under."

"A rock station," he continued, "provides plenty of interesting wild life. There are, for instance, the migrating birds . . . Hundreds of these, dazzled by its beam, would crash into the light and drop on the gallery. This is tragic for the birds but I saw no reason why they should not be turned to good purpose. Plucked and roasted, even the little ones made tasty dishes and added variety to our meals. Once a goose dropped from the heavens and, as you may guess, there was a bit of a celebration that day!"

Keeper Christie was at Gunfleet at the beginning of the Second World War when the water all around was heavily mined. He explained that Gunfleet Lighthouse was built on iron piles — an openwork structure on iron legs bedded deep in the sea bottom.

"Trinity House was afraid of the drifting mines becoming caught between the piles — and blowing us sky high," he said. "One small mine could have done the job easily at any moment, so Gunfleet was closed."

This was also the time when Nazi planes were dive bombing British lightships. Altogether an eventful life for someone who says nothing ever happens to him!

(Lee Chadwick)

Model Paper C

Questions on Passage 1   *Marks*

(a) Look at the typical kind of story told in Victorian times about lighthouses in lines 8–10.

Explain two general aspects of such stories which must have appealed to readers of that time?   **4 U**

(b) Explain how the sentence structure of lines 10–14 helps to reinforce the writer's ideas.   **4 U/A**

(c) How does the story of the incident in the Bahamas (lines 15–25) illustrate the meaning of "tragi-comic" (line 15)?   **4 U**

(d) Which aspects of the Flannan Islands story (lines 40–57) makes it unlikely that an explanation will ever be found?   **2 U**

(e) What are the different implications of "circulated" and "published" as used in the passage in line 52?   **2 U**

(f) What effect do the words "of course" have on the ending of paragraph 7, line 65?   **2 A**

(g) Explain the thinking behind the first appointment given to a new lighthouse keeper.   **2 U**

(h) How appropriate do you find the story of Edward Wood as a conclusion to this article?   **2 A/E**

(i) Look again at lines 58–80. Explain the qualifications, personal and professional, which are required of lighthouse keepers.   **8 U**

(30)

Questions on Passage 2

(j) Explain how effective you find the word choice and imagery in the first paragraph in creating the atmosphere.   **4 A/E**

(k) How does the sentence beginning "Nothing, however . . ." (line 9), act as a link between paragraphs 1 and 2?   **2 A**

Model Paper C

Marks

(l) Look again at paragraphs 4 and 5 (lines 16–23). How is contrast used in both paragraphs to emphasise the two points the writer is making about the lighthouse keeper's home? 4 U/A

(m) What are the essential duties of the lighthouse men as described in lines 32–36? 3 U

(n) (i) Explain the significance of the two sets of wild creatures mentioned in lines 56–63? 2 U

(ii) Explain your response to the way he tells the story of the goose in lines 65–66. 3 A/E

(o) Do you think the last sentence makes an effective ending to this reported interview? 2 A/E

(20)

Question on Both Passages

(p) Both passages try to make us aware of the nature of life on lighthouses. Explain, by comparing the two passages, which one you think achieves this purpose most effectively. You should consider content and style (sentence structure, word choice, imagery, etc.) in both passages in your answer. 10 A/E

(10)

Total = (60)

A = $18\frac{1}{2}$

U = 31

E = $10\frac{1}{2}$

HIGHER ENGLISH

MODEL PAPER D
Interpretation

NATIONAL QUALIFICATIONS

Time: 1 hour 30 minutes

You should attempt all questions.

The total value of the Paper is 60 marks.

INTERPRETATION

There are TWO passages and questions.

Read the passages carefully and then answer all the questions which follow. **Use your own words whenever possible and particularly when you are instructed to do so.**

You should read the passages to:

- understand what each writer has to say about Robert the Bruce (**Understanding — U**);

- analyse the choice of language, imagery and structures to show how they convey the writer's opinion about Bruce (**Analysis — A**);

- evaluate how effectively each writer has achieved his purpose (**Evaluation — E**).

A code letter (U, A, E) is used alongside each question to give some indication of the skills being assessed. The number of marks attached to each question will give some indication of the length and kind of answer required.

PASSAGE 1

In the first passage, the writer, J.B. Pick, reviews a new book about Robert the Bruce and comments on some of the ideas in it. In the second passage, Ronald McNair Scott describes the skirmishes which took place before the Battle of Bannockburn.

Tartan myth by design

Robert the Bruce: patriot or king of greed?

History is difficult country. Enclaves of sober records and official documents are surrounded by a forest of myth, rumour, and legend. Mediaeval chroniclers mixed fact with folk-tale. At times it is possible to test chronicle against chronicle, but a tone of honest candour is not enough to prove a story true: it shows only that the chronicler
5 believes what he says.

Robert the Bruce rivals King Arthur and Alfred of Wessex as a generator of legend. As the first Scottish Parliament for nearly 300 years gallops towards us at a lively pace, it is time to distinguish myth from midday and stand on solid ground. Was Robert de Brus, Earl of Carrick, an ambitious Norman land-holder squabbling with rival Norman
10 landholders for power and kingship, or was he a Scottish patriot fighting for freedom?

Was his underlying motive the desire to be king or a passion to achieve Scottish independence?

Caroline Bingham's exceptional clarity of aim and method enables her both to write a classic biography and to answer these questions without specifically asking them. By telling the story of Bruce's life with balanced insight, she also shows the emergence of the nation state in Europe, and the way opening for the replacement of conflicts between networks of feudal loyalties by conflicts first between bigwigs identifying themselves with nations, and eventually between peoples imbued with a sense of national identity.

It has been argued that the unjustified claim by Edward I of England to suzerainty over Scotland and his ruthless egoistic will to pursue the claim at all costs were chiefly responsible for forging the Scottish nation, while the determined struggle for liberation itself provided inspiration for developments in Europe.

Bingham starts by giving us a lucid picture of late-mediaeval society. The Normans brought to England by conquest, and to Scotland by royal invitation, a system of hierarchical fealty which involved every member of a Europe-wide ruling caste in a maze of conflicting loyalties. Edward I, for example, while claiming suzerainty over Scotland, gave homage to Philip IV of France for lands in Aquitaine, and repudiated that oath when it became convenient to do so. Both Bruces and Baliols had lands in England and Scotland. Where did their loyalties lie?

These two families laid claims of roughly equal validity to the throne of Scotland on the death of Alexander III. Edward I of England was brought in as a broker. He chose Baliol for diverse, devious reasons. The resulting feud between Bruces and Baliols ran on through generations.

When William Wallace rebelled against Edward's overweening claims to suzerainty, he did so in the name of King John Baliol. Robert the Bruce, on several occasions, swore fealty to Edward, and even set out to support him in arms, but the humiliation of Baliol was the humiliation of Scotland, and this he found unendurable. The manoeuvrings which followed were those of a man opposed both to the claims of Edward and to the kingship of Baliol, which placed him, in effect, at the third point of a triangle. They were also the manoeuvrings of one who, ambitious for kingship, was growing ever more deeply identified with the cause of an independent Scotland.

The twists and turns of this conflict of loyalties is an absorbing story, cogently and calmly told. Among the vital points Bingham makes are these: by the time that Robert the Bruce emerged as claimant to the throne, five generations of his family had lived in Scotland. The gradual transformation of allegiances is shown through language. Although landowners of Norman origin still spoke to each other in French, Robert, with Fergus of Galloway in his ancestry, spoke Gaelic and probably Scots, as well as having a working knowledge of Latin.

The struggle to gather an army, unite factions, invent tactics to counter superior force, and to steer a course through European and Papal politics, changed Bruce from a confused, ambitious, hot-tempered, determined maverick, into an able general with one clear, overriding aim — to achieve kingship without owing allegiance outside Scotland.

It is only possible, at this distance, to assess character through recorded action. Motives are hidden. But by any criteria Robert the Bruce was a man of remarkable courage, resource and resilience, able to react swiftly to changing circumstances, and yet able to stand back and see a picture whole. He was ruthless when necessary yet unusually generous to enemies. From whatever standpoint you look at him, Bruce emerges as one of the most redoubtable men of his day. No one else could have achieved independence for the Kingdom of Scotland at that time. What he could not achieve was lasting unity. The Highland clans continued with their own internecine concerns, and the nobility of Scotland retained an unmatched capacity for quarrelling among themselves.

What stays in my mind, after closing the book, are the reflections attributed by a chronicler to Andrew de Harday, Earl of Carlisle, who, in good faith, negotiated a general peace with Bruce, for which action he was accused of treason and executed by Edward II: "How much better it would be for the community of each realm if each King should possess his own kingdom freely and peacefully without any homage, instead of so many homicides, arsons, captivities, plunderings and raidings taking place every year." Common sense is uncommon at any period, particularly in the 14th century.

(J.B. Pick)

"Robert the Bruce" *by Caroline Bingham: Caroline Bingham examines the rise of Robert the Bruce from Earl of Carrick to King of Scots and the battle of Bannockburn, all set against a backdrop of generations of internecine feuding between Scottish lords. Reviewed by J.B. Pick.*

PASSAGE 2

Like many of the great commanders who followed him in history, Bruce took pains to make himself known to all his men, "ever, as he met them, he greeted them cheerfully, speaking an encouraging word to one or another and they, seeing their King welcome them in so forthright a manner, were greatly heartened and were ready to fight and die
5   to uphold his honour."

During this period he selected the site of the battlefield in which he would oppose the English. That which he chose was "almost the copybook military position for the strategic defence of Stirling Castle."

About two miles north of Torwood, the Roman road dipped down to the valley of the
10 Bannock burn. Rising in the hills to the west the burn descended through wooded slopes and meadows to the ford which served the road and then plunged into a deep gully by the hamlet of Bannock and cut its way through the boglands in an arc to the northeast to debouch into the Firth of Forth. North of this natural obstacle there was to the left of the road the New Park, a moderate area of undulating grassland backed by
15 thick woods which had been enclosed by Alexander III as a royal forest: to the right of the road a narrow stretch of meadow which ended abruptly at its eastern edge in a steep bank, dropping down into the Carse of Balquiderock, a flat plateau of clayland embraced by the arms of the Pelstream and the Bannock burn. Beyond these, marshlands, intersected by streams, extended to the Firth of Forth.

20 No advance by the English could be made from the east across this spongy area; nor could they make a detour to the west where the Torwood and the New Park stretched in an unbroken forest. Their only means of approach towards Stirling were along the Roman road through the New Park or somewhat to the east of the gully where by fording the Bannock burn where its banks were lower and taking the public track, they
25 could pass outside the New Park under the lea of the escarpment at the Carse's edge.

Bruce must have reconnoitred the ground on many occasions with his lieutenants for when the time came to take up their positions there the move was made with great smoothness. In the meantime, to prevent the English cavalry deploying onto the open ground either side of the Roman road, if they crossed the ford, he honeycombed the
30 area with pits dug a foot in breadth and knee deep camouflaged with brushwood and grass and had trees felled and placed in barricades across any tracks through the forest which might be accessible to horsemen.

While this work was being carried out he sent James Douglas and Sir Robert Keith with a small mounted patrol to monitor the progress of the English army.

35 On 22 June they returned with the news, which they reported to the King in private, that the English were on the move from Edinburgh in immense numbers, for the whole landscape was covered by mounted men with waving banners, columns of foot soldiers and archers and lines of wagons stretching into the distance. Never before had they seen such a multitude and splendour. Bruce told them to keep this knowledge to themselves
40 but to spread it abroad that the English were advancing in great disorder so that the men might not be discouraged.

Next morning, 23 June, soon after sunrise, the army heard Mass and prayed to God for their cause, and since it was the vigil of St John the Baptist they observed it as a fast, taking only bread and water. And when they had armed and taken their stations the King had it proclaimed to each division that if any were of faint heart let him depart at once, at which a great shout arose from the assembled troops that all would conquer or die.

As the English cavalry emerged from Torwood onto the green meadow which sloped down to the Bannock burn, their many coloured banners and armour glittering in the sun could be seen clearly from across the valley by the Scots who stood to arms.

The English vanguard came down across the meadow and their lines gradually contracted into a column as they approached the ford over the burn with the Earls of Hereford and Gloucester in the lead. The Earl of Hereford's nephew, Sir Henry de Bohun, rode some forty yards in front, clad in full armour on a powerful horse with his spear in his hand. As he came through the belt of trees on the north bank of the burn he saw on the open ground before him a single rider with an axe in his hand and a golden circlet around his helmet. Recognising the King of Scots, de Bohun without more ado couched his lance and spurred towards him.

Who knows what thoughts passed through Bruce's mind? The prudent course was to fall back within the ranks of his soldiers, but perhaps he was influenced by seeing the crest of the de Bohuns on the surcoat of his assailant. For it was to the de Bohuns that, when he was a fugitive, his lands in Annandale and Carrick had been handed over by Edward I, and it was to the de Bohuns that Edward II had given the Bruce domains in Essex. And then again, how could he, the victor in a hundred tournaments, retreat from such a challenge before the eyes of Scotsmen prepared to lay down their lives on his behalf? So he turned his horse and cantered towards de Bohun, and as the thunderous charge came near swerved to one side and rising in his stirrups brought down his axe with such force on his opponent's head that he cut through helmet, skull and brain and his axe handle shivered in two.

For a minute there was a stunned silence, and then with a wild cry the Highlanders of the King's division climbed over their fieldworks and charged on the English cavalry who were trying to line up on the open ground below, confused by the hidden pits into which many of them had fallen. The Earl of Gloucester was flung from his stumbling horse and only rescued by his squires and the rest took flight. Bruce stopped the pursuit at once, an eloquent tribute to his training, and brought his Highlanders back to their lines.

That evening Bruce held a conference with his chief commanders, whose experience of warfare enabled them to assess the enormous disparity between the two forces, to consider whether he should not make it his main objective to preserve the only Scottish army in being by retiring to the wild country of Lennox and beyond and leave starvation and the scorched earth to fight for him rather than risk the annihilation of Scotland's manhood. But while they were debating, Sir Alexander Seton, who was serving in the English army, came secretly to him through the night and said to Bruce, "Sir, if you ever intend to reconquer Scotland now is the time. The English have lost heart and are discouraged," and he pledged his life on pain of being hanged and drawn that if Bruce attacked them on the morrow he would surely win.

His description of the English army was accurate. So widespread was the defeatism that Edward II ordered his heralds to go to and fro throughout the army to explain that the events of the day had been mere skirmishes and that in the major battle to come victory
90 was certain and the rewards great.

(Ronald McNair Scott)

Questions on Passage 1

Marks

(a) Look carefully at paragraph 1. Explain how the writer continues the ideas contained in the image of "difficult country". — **4 A**

(b) By careful analysis of the sentence structure in paragraph 2 (lines 6–12), show how it assists his main argument. — **4 A/U**

(c) Look carefully at paragraph 4 (lines 20–23). Explain how what happened on a small scale in Scotland ended up influencing all of Europe. — **2 U**

(d) Look at paragraph 7 (lines 35–42). Explain the picture of Bruce's character which emerges from what the author tells us. — **4 U**

(e) Why does the writer give such emphasis to the importance of language in paragraph 8 (lines 43–49)? — **2 U**

(f) How effective do you find the sentence structure of paragraph 9 (lines 50–62) in conveying the writer's view? — **4 A/E**

(g) By the end of his wars, what had Bruce gained, and what had he failed to gain? — **3 U**

(h) How effective do you find the title of this newspaper article? — **1 E**

(i) Drawing information from lines 35–60, explain what Bruce had to do to achieve an independent Scotland and why, according to the writer, did he wish to achieve it? Use your own words. — **6 U**

(30)

Questions on Passage 2

(j) Explain the use of inverted commas in paragraph 1 (lines 1–5). — **1 A**

(k) By looking carefully at the first 4 paragraphs, explain what the writer means when he claims that the site Bruce chose was "almost the copybook military position for the defence of Stirling Castle"? — **3 U**

(l) Explain how the context helps you to arrive at the meaning of "reconnoitred", line 26. — **2 U**

(m) How does paragraph 6, lines 33–34, act as a linking device in the description of the events? — **2 A**

(n) Look carefully at the sentence structure of lines 35–39, "On 22 June . . . and splendour." How effectively would you say the sentence structure contributes to the impression the writer wishes to give of the English forces? — **4 A/E**

Model Paper D

Marks

(o) By examining the word choice in lines 51–58, show how the writer creates a contrast between the two men, Sir Henry de Bohun and Bruce, King of Scots. 4 A

(p) Look at lines 59–66. In no more than two sentences explain briefly two of the possible reasons for Bruce's action. 2 U

(q) In **your own words**, explain the two alternatives Bruce thought he was faced with before the arrival of Sir Alexander Seton. 2 U

(r) Explain the impression given of Edward II by the last paragraph? 2 A

(22)

Question on Both Passages

(s) If you wanted to stimulate someone else's interest in Robert the Bruce, which passage do you think would be most likely to do so?

Compare the passages in terms of ideas, stylistic features and point of view, etc. 8 E/A

(8)

Total =   (60)

A = 23

U = 28

E = 9

HIGHER ENGLISH	MODEL PAPER E Interpretation	NATIONAL QUALIFICATIONS

Time: 1 hour 30 minutes

You should attempt all questions.

The total value of the Paper is 60 marks.

INTERPRETATION

There are TWO passages and questions.

Read the passages carefully and then answer all the questions which follow. **Use your own words whenever possible and particularly when you are instructed to do so.**

You should read the passages to:

- understand what each writer has to say about hot air ballooning and its appeal to participants (**Understanding — U**);
- analyse the choice of language, imagery and structures to show how they convey the point of view and attitude to ballooning (**Analysis — A**);
- evaluate how effectively each writer has achieved his purpose (**Evaluation — E**).

A code letter (U, A, E) is used alongside each question to give some indication of the skills being assessed. The number of marks attached to each question will give some indication of the length and kind of answer required.

PASSAGE 1

In Passage 1 from the first chapter of Dick Brown's book, "Hot Air Ballooning", he gives a brief history of ballooning and explains what he thinks is its appeal. In Passage 2, Mick Brown, in his biography of Richard Branson, describes his balloon trip across the Atlantic from the USA to his landing in the sea off the coast of Scotland.

The Renaissance of Hot Air Ballooning

As a sport, hot air ballooning is a magical getaway. Whether skimming the tips of flowers along a country road or floating silently above the lazy pacing clouds, flight in a balloon is a fantasy voyage. It is a journey without a destination. It is an escape from the insensible rush of things. A chance to slow down, to suspend oneself in time and space, to simply unwind.

Ballooning's sense of freedom and detachment, both physical and mental, is a challenge to describe. Some say it is like sailing, but there is no wake. Others say it is like riding an elevator, but there is no top floor. Some say it is romantic, but not quite like falling in love. Almost everyone agrees that it is unlike any other form of aerial navigation. It is flight without wings. Man has devised no other machine quite so simple and uncluttered as a balloon, where riding invisible pathways blends a dreamlike serenity with a touch of nostalgia.

Using the time-honoured principle that hot air is lighter than cold air and that hot air rises, the sport is easy to comprehend. But ballooning came about quite by accident. In the early 1780s, the Montgolfier brothers stumbled upon the phenomenon of rising hot air as they observed paper ashes mysteriously float up a chimney. Although the phenomenon was probably discovered by earlier man, Joseph and Etienne Montgolfier are generally credited with the first practical application of hot air and the ensuing development of balloon flight. Incorrectly, however, the Montgolfier brothers reasoned that smoke had some mystical lifting power, and so early hot air balloons were fuelled with damp straw, old shoes, and brandy soaked rags.

The pioneering manned ascension by Francis Pilatre de Rosier and Marquis d'Arlandes in Paris on November 21, 1783, provided the spark which ignited man's revolutionary age of flight. But further progress in hot air ballooning was quelled by rapid developments in gas balloon flight. The smoke-belchers were replaced by hydrogen-filled balloons that offered increased lift and endurance. Gas balloons were used in science, war and sport during the 19th century, but then such aeronautics succumbed to powered flight. Increasingly more sophisticated winged contraptions, with their sputtering engines and intricate cockpit gadgetry, roared where silent balloons once drifted.

In the early 1960s, hot air ballooning experienced a dramatic revival, primarily due to improved materials and new technology. The development of strong, lightweight

Hot Air Ballooning by Dick Brown
Published by Tab Books © 1978
Reproduced with permission of The McGraw-Hill Companies.

synthetic fabrics combined with new flight control techniques featuring an onboard propane fuelled heater system to unleash a new era in balloon flight. The new burners had exceptionally high thermal outputs and offered a practical and economic means to keep the air hot and the balloon buoyant.

The development of the modern hot air balloon was stimulated by the US Navy, who solicited the balloon design and engineering expertise of Raven Industries of Sioux Falls, South Dakota. Raven, who had already pioneered in the building of helium-filled, onion-shaped polyethylene balloons for carrying scientific payloads to probe the upper atmosphere, went under contract to develop a small hot air balloon that could be employed in a balloon pilot training program for low altitude research by the Office of Naval Research. The Navy specified that the lift be provided by hot air because there was a need for a reusable balloon that was inexpensive and easy to operate. The gas balloon had neither feature. There has always been a high premium on hydrogen and helium gas. But hot air is free except for the minimal cost of fuel for a propane burner to heat the air. Simplicity of operation was an important design constraint. The manual labour of getting the gas balloon in the air is strenuous and time-consuming and the valving and ballasting necessary to sustain flight in a gas balloon is a severe limitation in aircraft manoeuvrability. Consequently, Raven Industries developed the "Vulcoon", a name derived not from vulcanized synthetic fabric but from the mythical god of fire.

Modern hot air ballooning made its debut on October 22, 1960, when Ed Yost lifted off the ground in a 40,000 cubic foot balloon near Sioux Falls. He sustained thermal flight for nearly one-half hour — a remarkable achievement after so many years of inactivity for hot air ballooning.

Although born of a military requirement, the modern hot air balloon nearly died when that requirement was suddenly cancelled by the Navy. It was rejuvenated when a few Raven engineers recognised the potential market for a sports version of the military model. Improvements in design and operation came rapidly after Ed Yost's inaugural flight. His efforts were soon complemented by those of two other distinguished balloon designers — Don Piccard and Tracy Barnes.

The hot air balloon, although no longer called a Vulcoon, survives as the simplest of flying machines. It is a massive, unwieldy craft that simply cannot be rushed. While it willingly responds to the whims of the wind, it begrudgingly responds to the desires of the pilot. Its resistance to changes in vertical and lateral movement, coupled with its inherent slow response when it does move, adds a special dimension to the sport and a unique challenge to the pilot.

People of romantic sensibilities are easily overcome by the excitement and curiosity of a brightly coloured balloon. They become enraptured by the thrill and hopelessly addicted to the charms of this gentle pastime — this magnetic sport. Coaxed by invisible zephyrs, each flight is an adventure, with the final landing spot unknown until the end of the flight.

The challenge of balloon flight is not simply to drift along at the mercy of the wind, but to explore different pathways across an ocean which is layered with different air

75 currents, and for the balloonist, this means different courses to follow. Consequently, steering can be achieved to a limited extent by searching for varying winds at different altitudes. While the wind provides direction to a flight, and carries a balloon along with it, there is little sensation of being in the wind because a balloon offers essentially no resistance to the wind.

80 The pilot must decide in advance where he wants to go and what, if anything, he must do to get there. He must anticipate the influence of subtle weather disturbances which almost always are invisible to him. He must plan ahead because when decisions are made, they are not easily reversed. He cannot circle around and try again. Commitments rarely permit reconsideration. What little control the pilot has, he must
85 use wisely or his balloon will quickly become a plaything of the wind.

The hot air balloon has a mind of its own, never submitting to total domination, never relinquishing all control, and thus presenting a continuous challenge to those who seek sporting excitement and free-spirited adventure.

(Dick Brown)

PASSAGE 2

On Wednesday, the day before the Virgin Atlantic Flyer balloon was scheduled to take off, two lawyers arrived at the door of Richard Branson's hotel suite and were ushered inside. They left an hour later, carrying a signed copy of Branson's last will and testament. That morning the capsule was tipped on its side, resting on a yellow
5   inflatable cushion, in a position to be attached to the envelope (the balloon) itself. Gingerly, the folded envelope was taken from its container, unfurled and spread across the green. Inflating the balloon was always going to be one of the most hazardous aspects of the entire operation. It could be inflated once, and only once. A tear, a snag on a tree or piece of equipment and the whole project could be aborted. It required
10 nothing less than absolute calm.

As darkness descended, inflation of the envelope began. At three a.m. on the Thursday morning, the car carrying Branson and Lindstrand from their hotel moved slowly through the darkness towards the site, a blue light flashing on its roof. The night sky was perfectly still and quiet. The car turned a corner, from behind a screen of trees,
15 before sloping down to the site. "Christ!" Branson breathed. "Can you stop the car?" What he saw made his heart suddenly beat faster. In front of them, the balloon filled their entire field of vision; picked out by spotlights, vast and eerie, an enormous shining black orb strained at its tether, as below it the burners breathed fire into its gaping mouth. Orange-suited figures swarmed purposefully around its base, and
20 disembodied voices echoed from the public address system through the woodland. Nobody spoke as the car edged forward slowly, to be engulfed in a tide of pointing cameras and lights and jabbering voices.

With the first glimmer of dawn painting an orange rim along the mountain range to the east, the countdown began. As the heat of the burners gained in intensity, the balloon,
25 with Branson and Lindstrand in it, lifted inches from the ground, then hovered, checked in its progress by the ballast of sandbags hanging from its side. Around it, hands tugged at the guy lines to set the balloon free. Then suddenly something went wrong. A line snagged around two fuel tanks and, with pulling, brought them crashing to the ground. The capsule rocked slightly, keeled as if about to plunge to the ground,
30 then righted itself and rose slowly upwards. It skirted the trees, hung in the air and then, as if pushed by a giant finger, rolled across the crimson sky, like a giant ballbearing, glinting in the strengthening sun.

Within six hours they had covered 420 nautical miles (500 statute miles), and the balloon was skimming through the sky at an incredible 110–120 knots, a mote in the jet
35 stream, straining to climb higher as the solar skin yielded to the warmth of the sun. Branson and Lindstrand grinned at each other in disbelief. Things were going better than either of them had dared to hope. There was no sound, no untoward movement in the capsule. They were aware of the extraordinary sensation of being cradled in the sky; utterly safe and secure. Far below, the land slipped quickly by, like scenery being
40 wound across a stage; on every side it was shining blue into infinity. Branson got a start when he looked behind the capsule and could see a plume of white smoke trailing across the sky behind them. For a moment he thought the balloon was on fire, then realised it was simply a vapour trail caused by the balloon arriving in the bitterly cold air at 27,000 feet. Between Halifax, Nova Scotia, and St John's, Newfoundland, there was a sudden

jerk and the balloon pulled upwards. For a fleeting moment, Lindstrand thought they had collided with something, but a few seconds later the radio crackled with a message from a passing Concorde. The plane had flown by 28,000 feet above, but in the thin atmosphere its sonic boom shock-wave had shaken the balloon like a giant hand. Three more Concordes would pass by in the course of the flight, but all radioed in advance.

Throughout the night and into the following morning, a procession of passenger jets flew past, out of sight, but within radio distance. The Virgin Atlantic Jumbo Jet carrying the balloon's launch and recovery crew and the two pilots' families back to Britain descended 4,000 feet to fly a figure of eight around the balloon. In the capsule, Eve Branson's voice came crackling over the receiver with a laugh. "Can't you go any faster, Ricky?"

At 2.33 p.m. on the afternoon of Friday 3 July the balloon crossed the coast of Ireland, over Donegal. They had been airborne for just 29 hours and 23 minutes.

They began to consider the prospect of landing. The astonishing speed of their journey across the Atlantic had created an unforeseen problem; only two double fuel tanks had been used during the flight; three full tanks were still attached to the capsule. These would have to be jettisoned before landing to minimise the risk of an explosion. But how to get rid of them was a problem. Below them was a solid base of cloud; to drop the tanks by parachute was to risk inadvertently hitting something, or someone. Even dropping them in water would be like laying mines. The men decided they would descend gently, deposit the tanks on land and climb on towards the Scottish mainland. Lindstrand ignited the burners and began shooting bursts of hot air into the envelope to control its rate of descent. Through the break in the cloud, they could see Londonderry airfield, but ahead was only open farmland. The wind was much faster at ground level than they had anticipated. The balloon tore across a field, gouging and skimming the grass, then veered upwards, missing the top of a barn by feet, and climbed sharply away, leaving its remaining fuel canisters buried in the grass below. There had been no need to jettison the tanks; they had been torn off in the impact.

Stripped of the weight of the surplus fuel, the balloon soared sharply upwards. Branson and Lindstrand were both shaken by the incident. The impact had knocked out all electrical power in the balloon; the lights were dead; most importantly, so was the radio. Branson wanted to turn on the emergency beacons each man carried in his pocket, but Lindstrand argued against it; it would only make everyone more anxious. They were going to bring the balloon down. Branson switched his on anyway, but it too was dead. Everything was going horribly wrong.

(Mick Brown)

Model Paper E

Questions on Passage 1

Marks

(a) Look carefully at the first paragraph, lines 1–5. By close reference to the word choice and sentence structure, explain what impression of ballooning the writer is trying to create.
3 A

(b) Explain whether you think the writer's use of images and comparisons in paragraph 2, lines 6–12, is effective in explaining the appeal of ballooning.
3 A/E

(c) Look carefully at lines 26–30. How does the writer bring out the contrast in his view between balloons and aeroplanes?
4 A

(d) Explain briefly what the great advantage was that the "Vulcoon" had over the gas filled balloons which meant it fulfilled the US Navy demands.
3 U

(e) Look carefully at paragraph 9, lines 62–67. Why does the writer conclude this paragraph with the claim that ballooning is "a unique challenge to the pilot"?
4 U

(f) "zephyrs" (line 70). By using the general context of paragraphs 9, 10 and 11 (lines 62–79), say how the context helps you to arrive at the meaning of this word.
2 U

(g) By looking carefully at the sentence structure, word choice and imagery of the last paragraph, explain whether you think is makes a good conclusion to the passage.
4 A/E

(h) By looking carefully at paragraphs 11–13 (lines 73–88), explain in your own words to what extent a pilot can control his balloon in the air.
6 U

(29)

Questions on Passage 2

(i) Why does the writer refer to Richard Branson's will before describing the balloon flight?
1 U

(j) Which word in paragraph 1, lines 1–10, makes clear how carefully the balloon is treated?
1 U/A

(k) Look at lines 16–22. By analysing at least two phrases in the sentence beginning, "In front of them . . .", explain why Branson's "heart suddenly beat faster".
4 A

(l) By looking carefully at the sentence structure and word choice of lines 29–32, describing the beginning of the flight, explain how it contributes to the tone the writer uses to describe this moment.
4 A/E

Model Paper E

Marks

(m) Explain the cause of two moments of alarm as they were crossing the Atlantic in paragraph 4 (lines 33–49).   **4 U**

(n) Explain whether you think the inclusion of Eve Branson's comment (lines 54–55) adds to the mood of the passage or not.   **2 E**

(o) How does the context help you to define the meaning of "jettisoned" in line 61?   **2 U**

(p) How does the word choice and imagery emphasise the danger in lines 69–72.   **4 A**

(22)

Question on Both Passages

(q) After reading the two passages, explain which most successfully made you feel the appeal of ballooning.

Compare the two passages in terms of their main ideas and such stylistic features as point of view, tone, imagery, structure, etc.   **9 E/A**

(9)

Total = (60)

$A = 25\frac{1}{2}$

$U = 22\frac{1}{2}$

$E = 12$

HIGHER ENGLISH

MODEL PAPER F
Interpretation

NATIONAL QUALIFICATIONS

Time: 1 hour 30 minutes

You should attempt all questions.

The total value of the Paper is 60 marks.

INTERPRETATION

There are TWO passages and questions.

Read the passages carefully and then answer all the questions which follow. **Use your own words whenever possible and particularly when you are instructed to do so.**

You should read the passages to:

- understand what the writers have to say about the film "The Exorcist" and its appeal to audiences (**Understanding — U**);

- analyse the choice of language, imagery and structures to show how they convey their points of view and contribute to the impact of the film (**Analysis — A**);

- evaluate how effectively each writer has achieved his purpose (**Evaluation — E**).

A code letter (U, A, E) is used alongside each question to give some indication of the skills being assessed. The number of marks attached to each question will give some indication of the length and kind of answer required.

PASSAGE 1

In the first passage, taken from 'The Scotsman' newspaper, Trevor Johnston looks at the effect the film "The Exorcist" had on audiences 25 years ago, considers its rerelease in the cinema and weighs up the reasons for its still not being available on video. In the second passage, writer and critic Mark Kermode analyses some of the film techniques used in "The Exorcist".

Be afraid. Be very afraid.

Back in the cinemas after 25 years, "The Exorcist" has lost none of its power. Why not, asks **Trevor Johnston**.

It is Boxing Day, 1973, in New York City. It is cold: temperatures are below freezing. Altogether it is a day to be at home in the warm. But outside the movie theatres, queues begin to form in the middle of the morning. What are they so keen to see? Paul Newman? Robert Redford? In fact the film has no major stars. It is the story of a young
5 girl from Maryland, who becomes possessed by the Devil. It is "The Exorcist".

It was then, and for its millions of devotees it remains, the scariest film ever made, a reputation that will be put to the test when it is re-released, in pristine new prints, in Scotland from Friday.

Almost 25 years on from its first appearance, does "The Exorcist" still have the power
10 to put the fear of God into us? It is certainly a film whose reputation precedes it. Reports of American cinemas sweeping the vomit from the aisles whipped up anticipation before the film hit Britain in March, 1974. The St John's Ambulance Service was put on duty in London's West End, while the National Festival of Light, Mary Whitehouse's censorship group, set up its own emergency helpline to console
15 disturbed viewers. Almost anyone who grew up in the Seventies will have some story about a cousin who fainted or a friend's friend who lost their lunch outside the cinema.

Approved uncut for the cinema, "The Exorcist" has effectively been banned on video in Britain since the 1984 Video Recordings Act regulated the so-called "video nasties" then allowed free rein. A new generation has grown up not knowing anything about it.

20 "The problem with 'The Exorcist' is not that it's a bad film," says James Perman, Secretary of the British Board of Film Classification since 1975, "It's that it's a very good film. It's one of the most powerful films ever made. And it's that very power which is the problem on video, where you are importing it into children's homes. We had to ask ourselves: 'If this film is seen by under-age kids would it be so terrifying that
25 it would seriously disturb them?'"

So what is it about "The Exorcist" that has the censors running scared and spectators ducking under their cinema seats? It was hardly the first hit movie to confront the Devil himself. "Rosemary's Baby", the Roman Polanski thriller, and even "The Devil Rides Out", Hammer's version of the Dennis Wheatley bestseller, could already claim that
30 distinction. What was different about "The Exorcist" is that it tackled the issue of demonic possession almost as if the film were a documentary.

"It's not a story about the 15th century or the Dark Ages; it's a contemporary film that is presented straightforwardly and realistically," reflects William Friedkin, the film's director, who has supervised the forthcoming reissue, happy to restore the battered original negative and upgrade the spooky soundtrack to digital stereo. "It doesn't have its tongue in its cheek like the old Hammer horrors. It is presented as something which is possible, which is occurring. And the fact that people are moved by it means they believe it."

And what we believe in is indeed a truly disturbing case history. While her actress mother, Chris MacNeil (Ellen Burstyn), works on her latest movie, Regan, her 12 year old daughter, played by Linda Blair, begins to be overcome by a mysterious condition. At first she thrashes about uncontrollably on her bed, before the bed itself starts moving around of its own accord.

Soon a guttural voice that is not her own begins mouthing obscenities, blasphemous language that is soon to be accompanied by gross facial distortions and telekinetic side-effects. With the doctors baffled, Burstyn calls on the help of a Jesuit priest, a specialist in psychological counselling, who witnesses yet more inexplicable phenomena — a gush of vomited green bile and the "child" displaying personal knowledge of his own family to which she would have had no access.

Those who saw a recent BBC documentary will know that Ms Blair's revolving head was, in fact a dummy tested for macabre effectiveness by a surreptitious night-time excursion in the front seat of a New York cab. That the horrible creaking sound as the head turned through 360 degrees was made by crumpling a leather wallet into the microphone. That the vapours of breath coming from the actors' mouths during the crucial exorcism sequence were achieved by refrigerating the entire set well below zero.

And that the performers' shocked expressions can often be attributed to Friedkin's habit of firing blanks from his guns without warning.

Although all the effects still look persuasive, even when set beside their computer generated Nineties equivalents, it is the combination of the film's shock tactics, with its serious underlying religious implications that may be the key to its uniquely haunting potency.

While many critics expressed revulsion at the film when it was first released, perhaps surprisingly, it received strong support from publications such as *The Catholic News* which called it "deeply spiritual" and said that it was "refreshing to see an honest film about good and evil as supernatural realities."

"The Exorcist" long since has proven its power over believers and non-believers alike. The courage of the priests in facing up to the terrifying powers of darkness armed only with a sprinkling of holy water and a few ardent recitations is one of recent cinema's most unequivocal and unironic expressions of faith, enough to sway the waverers (if only momentarily) in the context of the film's escalating anxieties.

Friedkin himself, speaking from his Los Angeles office, where he has a statement from the BBFC's James Ferman in front of him, is obviously rankled that the film is still not available for home viewing in the UK. "He's concerned that a bunch of teenage girls are going to see the film and it's somehow going to freak them out. There's an argument to

75 be made for that, but I don't think it's the responsibility of the state to decide what anyone is going to watch, either in a public place or in their own homes. That is the responsibility of parents and a responsibility they must not shirk. A child should not be allowed to see 'The Exorcist' on their own, but what about the many households where there are no children. They are forbidden to see it on video and I find that ludicrous."

80 In the wake of the whole "video nasties" debacle and ongoing concerns over the potential (but as yet unproven) links between screen violence and anti-social behaviour, it seems unlikely in the near future that the position of the BBFC regarding "The Exorcist" on video will change. However much that might irritate the film's adult aficionados, it does give Warner Brothers a strong marketing angle as they gear the film
85 up for its Scottish release. It is some measure of its continuing contentiousness, however, that they are only releasing it in Scotland at this stage. For the rest of Britain it is still wait-and-see.

Twenty-five years on, they will surely be hoping that "The Exorcist" still has the power to turn heads. And not just on the big screen.

(Trevor Johnston)

PASSAGE 2

"The Exorcist" by Mark Kermode from BFI Modern Classics

"The Exorcist" opens with the atmospheric Northern Iraq prologue which Blatty had once so fiercely defended, then later doubted and omitted from his original screenplay. Shot not by Owen Roizman (the film's director of photography elsewhere) but by cameraman Billy Williams, this haunting curtain raiser establishes a number of aural
5 and visual motifs which will reverberate throughout the movie. Over red-on-black titles, a discordant screeching sound offers an eerie pre-echo of the creaking bedsprings and demonic scratching that will later infest Regan MacNeil's Georgetown bedroom. As the atonal screech cuts into the clearly heard Arabic prayer, the credits give way to an image of a huge ochre sun, burning over the ruins of Nineveh. A young boy is seen
10 leaping across the gullies of a vast archaeological dig, the rapid motion of his legs criss-crossing the screen which itself seems to shimmer with an almost stroboscopic pulse. All around the dig, picks are driven into the dirt-belching earth, creating a dysrhythmic throb which will be re-established a few minutes later by workmen clanging hammers on an anvil in a hellishly sweaty forge. The sound itself will be heard again during the
15 exorcism itself, blended among the barrage of creaks and groans which lend the ritual such force.

As the camera peers through the young boy's spindly legs, foreshadowing the coming grotesque views of Regan MacNeil, Father Lankester Merrin (Max von Sydow) is told in Arabic that "They found something . . . small pieces" at the base of the mound.
20 Sifting through a collection of lamps, arrowheads and coins, Merrin notices what appears to be a St Joseph medal and observes bemusedly, "This is strange . . ." Although little is made of Merrin's find, Friedkin has already subtly introduced us to the magical cinematic talisman which will mysteriously reappear throughout the movie without narrative explanation, linking apparently disparate characters and events. The
25 discovery of a Christian medal buried in pre-Christian pagan rock (Merrin's next find is a green stone amulet in the figure of the demon Pazuzu) serves too as a symbol of the coming battle not only between good and evil, but also between past and present.

Merrin's journeys to and from the dig through the streets of Mosul are littered with allusions to the coming horrors — from the blind eye of a steel worker which prefigures
30 Regan's demonic eyerolling, to the haggard face of an old woman which eerily resembles that of the ravaged child. As Merrin climbs the mound to confront the giant statue of the demon Pazuzu, angry dogs snarl and scuffle in the dust, providing an aggressive aural accompaniment to Merrin's "High Noon"-style stand-off with an ancient enemy.

35 As the prologue climaxes, the sound of the raging dogs gives way to the snarl of modern traffic as we dissolve to a view across the Potomac and a slow zoom towards the Georgetown house of Chris MacNeil (Ellen Burstyn). In her bedroom, a bedside lamp is switched on in close-up, the sudden electric glow mimicking the slow-burning dawn sun of Nineveh which opened the movie. It is here that Chris first hears the scraping
40 sounds from the attic, a series of arrythmic clumps which seem to have spilled over from the prologue. In a brilliantly compressed introduction, which seems on the surface

to have little narrative import, Friedkin has conjured an ancient, exotic battleground between good and evil, and injected it directly into the home of a modern, wealthy, single, white mother with no apparent religious connections. The scene has also been set for the forthcoming contest between science and religion, in which doctors and priests will battle to subdue an uncontrollable child whose sociopathic behaviour is threatening to destroy her already vulnerable family.

Perhaps the most memorable image in William Friedkin's film of "The Exorcist" is that of the shadowy figure of Father Merrin, arriving outside the house in Prospect Street, gazing up at the unearthly light which illuminates the night fog in a phosphorescent haze. Interpreting Blatty's writing through eyes sharpened by the paintings of Magritte, Friedkin constructs a hauntingly inverted image in which Merrin (the messenger of good) is depicted as a dark, brooding presence, captured in a radiant blaze emanating from Regan's bedroom (the seat of evil), reminding us of Lucifer's designation as "the bearer of light". Not only does this iconographic frieze perfectly capture the paradoxical power of Blatty's novel, it also symbolises the ongoing struggle between good and evil which Friedkin's movie would leave open ended. Crucially, it is an image not of closure, but of anticipation — of Merrin arriving at the scene of a battle which is inevitable yet unexpected, foretold yet undetermined.

In remembering the filming of "The Exorcist", two themes were repeatedly touched upon by the participants. The first was the tense atmosphere on set which many sources attributed to Friedkin's use of disturbing noises — from human groans and the grunts of tree frogs to the taped cries of a genuine exorcism — to generate a sense of otherworldly unease during shooting. Equally popular were tales of the "indestructible disposition" of the young star Linda Blair, whose work on "The Exorcist" continues to impress all those who were involved with the film, and whose even-tempered patience remains a source of bafflement to her elders. "I had a very removed experience of both the film and the 'creature' I portrayed," Blair now remembers:

"I honestly never saw the horror in 'The Exorcist'. I never saw the devil. A lot of it I just didn't understand at the time. I remember when we got into the demon stages, there were many occasions when Billy would take me up to his office and say, 'O.K. now here's a piece of paper with tomorrow's new dialogue on it.' And I'd sit on the couch and read it and go, 'Billy, this is awful. I can't say that!' And he'd just go, 'Yeah, yeah you can . . .' and you know, he has a way of making people do things. So I just got on with it."

(Mark Kermode)

Model Paper F

Questions on Passage 1

Marks

(a) Look carefully at the sentence structure of paragraph 1 (lines 1–5) and explain how it contributes to the author's argument. — 4 A/U

(b) Look at lines 9–16 and explain what kind of problems are anticipated when "The Exorcist" is shown. — 4 U

(c) Explain carefully James Perman's argument for not allowing a video of "The Exorcist" to be released. — 4 U

(d) What is suggested about Hammer horror movies by the expression "tongue in its cheek" (line 36)? — 2 A/U

(e) Explain how one of the special effects was achieved. — 2 U

(f) Look at paragraph 12 (lines 56–57). Comment on its structure and explain whether you think it is effective. — 3 A/E

(g) Explain the use of the word "unironic" as used in line 69. — 2 A/U

(h) Explain carefully James Friedman's views on the refusal of the BBFC to permit a video of "The Exorcist" to be released. — 3 U

(i) Comment on the effectiveness of the final paragraph as a conclusion to this article. — 2 E

(j) Drawing your information from lines 20–70, explain what, according to Trevor Johnston and others, makes "The Exorcist" a good film which will always appeal to audiences. Use your own words as far as possible. — 6 U

(32)

Questions on Passage 2

(k) By looking carefully at word choice in paragraph 1, explain how the writer helps us to imagine the sound effects in the opening sequence of the film "The Exorcist". — 4 A/U

(l) Look at lines 17–24. Explain the symbolic importance of the St Joseph's medal in both the prologue and the rest of the film. — 2 U

(m) "As the prologue climaxes . . . house of Chris MacNeil (Ellen Burstyn)." (lines 35–37). Explain how this sentence acts as a link in the structure of the article. — 2 A

Model Paper F

Marks

(n) Look carefully at the imagery in lines 31–47. By analysing at least two examples, explain what they suggest about the mood of the film. 3 A

(o) How does paragraph 6 explain the meaning of "paradoxical" as used in line 56. 3 A/U

(p) Do you think that the comments of Linda Blair, the young actress who played the part of Regan, the girl possessed, make a good conclusion to this extract? 4 E

(18)

QUESTIONS ON BOTH PASSAGES

(q) Which passage do you think makes the film "The Exorcist" sound the more interesting?

Compare the two passages in terms of ideas, attitudes and stylistic features such as point of view, tone, imagery, structure, etc. 10 A/E

(10)

Total =   (60)

A = 19

U = $28\frac{1}{2}$

E = $12\frac{1}{2}$

MODEL PAPER G

HIGHER ENGLISH **Interpretation** **NATIONAL QUALIFICATIONS**

Time: 1 hour 30 minutes

You should attempt all questions.

The total value of the Paper is 60 marks.

INTERPRETATION

There are TWO passages and questions.

Read the passages carefully and then answer all the questions which follow. **Use your own words whenever possible and particularly when you are instructed to do so.**

You should read the passages to:

- understand what the writers have to say about department stores and shopping centres (**Understanding — U**);

- analyse the choice of language, imagery and structures to show how they convey his / her point of view and contribute to our understanding of the atmosphere in these stores (**Analysis — A**);

- evaluate how effectively each writer has achieved his / her purpose (**Evaluation — E**).

A code letter (U, A, E) is used alongside each question to give some indication of the skills being assessed. The number of marks attached to each question will give some indication of the length and kind of answer required.

PASSAGE 1

In the first passage, the author, Alison Adburgham, in the last chapter of her book "Shops and Shopping 1800–1914", looks at the big department stores as they were at the beginning of the century and considers the aims of their creators and the atmosphere they hoped to create in their stores. In the second passage, the writer, Charles Clover, looks at the way the developers of modern Shopping Centres use the services of experts to ensure that the atmosphere in their stores is absolutely right.

STORES REACH THEIR ZENITH

As the reign of King Edward soared to its zenith, extravagance was the prevailing mood of Society, with mature and triumphant womanhood the focus of all glory, laud, and bonheur. With a middle-aged but still pleasure-loving king, and a middle-aged but still beautiful queen, the age of conquest was raised and the horizons of flirtation extended.
5 "Oh, these Edwardian women!" recalls Frederick Willis. "To see them in their glory one had to be in Old Bond Street between the hours of four and six in the afternoon. The street was full of their carriages, and there was an air of reverence in the shops as they entered. On the stage they were represented in every musical comedy. No matter where the setting of the play might be, Hong Kong, Arcadia, or Floradora, there they
10 were among the palms and mimosa, and described on the programme as 'English visitors'. All they had to do was to wear the most expensive gowns, look delightfully bored and majestically useless. We fawned upon them; they ruled the world with a gentle wave of a delicately gloved hand; they were omnipotent. They achieved their prestige simply by putting the accent on femininity. We were charmed or terrified by
15 their mystery and aloofness."

This hot-house, conservatory atmosphere was exactly right for the growth, burgeoning, and blossoming of fashion shops. And in Wigmore Street, Debenham & Freebody, like the divinities they served, reached a splendid maturity of prosperity and prestige. In 1907 they completed their handsome new building, which was in far better taste than
20 the routine "French Renaissance style" which had been the accepted and expected architectural expression of the grand emporiums of the late Victorians. In the following year, a Franco-British Exhibition was held in London, and Debenhams issued a souvenir booklet for visitors to their stores:

"You may visit the various departments, then, if you wish, have lunch or tea at very
25 moderate charges in the quiet, elegant Restaurant, to which a Smoking-room and Gentlemen's Cloakroom are attached. The Ladies' Club Room, which adjoins a luxuriously appointed suite of Dressing and Retiring Rooms, is open to lady visitors, who may there read the papers and magazines, telephone, write letters, or meet their friends. Parcels and letters may be addressed to the Cloak Room."

30 The appointments of the whole store were of a restrained but rich solidity, and although reticence kept the details out of this souvenir booklet, there never was a more comfortably contrived Ladies' Room, with its range of separate retiring rooms, each one containing a dressing-table and mirror, a marble wash basin, tessellated walls. Mahogany seating completed the sanitary fitments which bore the name of "The

Cavendish". Was this a happy coincidence or by special arrangement to tie up with the original Cavendish House? This Ritz of retiring rooms remained exactly as then until the alterations of 1964.

Meanwhile Harrods had grown from small beginnings as a grocery and provision shop into an immense emporium faced with Doulton's terra-cotta, having eighty departments with a thirty-six acre shopping area, in which the variety of merchandise justified the telegraphic address of EVERYTHING, LONDON.

The year that Harrods reached their diamond jubilee was the year when Gordon Selfridge opened his great emporium in Oxford Street. And Harrods chose the actual week of Selfridge's highly dramatized inauguration to put on a series of jubilee concerts. These concerts were decorous, dignified affairs, with Landon Ronald conducting the London Symphony Orchestra. Selfridge must surely have been speaking sarcastically when he said Harrods had "put up a magnificent counterblast to our opening". His own blast was given by an army trumpeter blowing a fanfare from the first-floor parapet above the main entrance as the Selfridge flag was unfurled.

Not even Selfridge, the social climber from the new world with small knowledge of London society, can have expected that fashionable women would spend a day at Selfridges — not those aloof and intimidating Edwardian creatures described by Frederick Willis. The customers he envisaged were of the great new middle and lower middle classes. These might equally well afford to spend a day at Harrods, and would find the amenities equal to those that Selfridge was offering to them, if not better — but they were shy of strolling into Harrods just to have a look round and use the public services. In contrast, when they walked along Oxford Street they were irresistibly sucked into Selfridges.

Gordon Selfridge's biographer, Reginald Pound, sums up Selfridge's influence on the retail trade of England after his first five years, that is on the eve of the 1914 war: "He could claim to have been a transforming influence on the world of retail selling, to have accomplished greater changes in the shopping life of the metropolis than any of his rivals. He would rather lose business than give shoppers the impression that the store existed only to sell them goods, which was the old way. 'I want them to enjoy the warmth and light, the colours and styles, the feel of fine fabrics. That is the basis of this business'; and it was a new basis. He had completely revolutionised store organization, layout and display. He had introduced new methods in staff training which had brought round him what was probably the ablest body of workers in the distributive trades and certainly one of the most loyal."

The attractions of a big store, whether it was Lewis's in Market Street, or Selfridges in Oxford Street, were irresistible to a generation which had few entertainments. More and more women of all classes were beginning to earn money of their own before marriage and, after marriage, to have control over the family purse. The growth of the stores can be seen to run parallel with the social emancipation of women — their emancipation from the restrictions of inhibiting home life, from their dependence upon father or husband for money to spend, and from the tyranny of private dressmakers and their interminable fittings.

Goodwill, that intangible but invaluable asset, was something which flowed both ways: goodwill from the shopkeeper to the customer surged back as customer goodwill to the shop. There was a *rapport*. A shop is more than a building, fittings, stock and staff, particularly a shop where clothes are bought. So much of the heart, so many high hopes, so many hesitations, go into the purchase of personal adornment that where there is a sympathetic atmosphere, an ambience of interest and understanding, someone who knows your name, that is the shop to which you return again and again. The human element is a factor too elusive to be assessed by accountancy and remote control. Especially is it incalculable when dealing with those two most capricious of customers, women and fashion.

(Alison Adburgham)

PASSAGE 2

Persuading Us To Shop Till We Drop
Too many roundabouts, he has found, are stressful for women

David Peek knows what it takes to make consumers part with their money. **Charles Clover** discovers some of the tricks.

Beggared and exhausted by the Christmas binge? Trying to avoid the false economies of the January sales? Never want to darken a shop door again? So far so good, but watch out when the urge to splurge returns. There are people planning to make self-restraint even more difficult in 1999.

5   Bears may rampage through the stock markets, but high priests of consumerism still believe that by studying shoppers' needs and satisfying them better, smart retailers can go on parting customers from their painfully-acquired cash.

One such shopping guru is David Peek, "consumer behaviourist" and consultant to the developers of Bluewater, Europe's largest shopping and leisure destination which opens
10 on March 16 off the M2 near Dartford in Kent.

An environmentalist's nightmare, Bluewater will have 1·5 million square feet of shop floor, 300 retailers, 6,500 staff, a car park with 13,000 spaces and an expected turnover of £650 million a year.

Peek and his wife, Sonia, have built a niche advising architects and designers of
15 shopping centres what makes customers switch their loyalty from an existing store and travel 10, 20 or 40 miles to a new one — and how to avoid designs, layouts and materials that make them edgy and want to flee before their credit cards have been swiped.

There are two fundamental questions when it comes to building a shopping centre, he says. First, is the money there? Second — and this is where David Peek Associates
20 comes in — how do *we* get it, as opposed to somebody else? The answer is to make people feel "comfortable and enthusiastic about the proposition".

Increasingly, as shoppers become more discerning and competition increases, this means focusing on intangible things such as safety, air quality, light and choice of materials — what Peek calls "total sensory design" — as well as perennially important
25 things such as value and service.

He recently chided a leading store for having the smell of mulligatawny from the restaurant wafting through the ladies' lingerie. He said it was the equivalent of a showroom full of dirty cars.

"Ten years ago," says Peek, "we could sell a shopping centre on the proposition: cold
30 in summer, warm in winter, never rains. Not any more. Once people used to compare shops in the nearest town, or the town next door. Now they say I like Barcelona very much and I think Milan's coming on. I'm talking about quite ordinary, not very well-off people."

Shops now compete with duty-free shopping and the Internet. Your competitor may be in Tennessee. You may not know he exists. Shops also compete with other growing calls on our residual spending, such as cheap foreign travel. Cheap flights mean shopping centres compete globally. People go to New York for £150 to do their Christmas shopping.

This, says Peek, is not as daft as it sounds. Peek, who works in the United States, as well as France, Spain and Ireland, knows that British shoppers pay premium prices for branded goods which more ruthless American shoppers simply wouldn't tolerate. So you can buy a pair of Timberland shoes, a Burberry mac and save most if not all your Virgin air fare *and have a good time*. You have to compete with that.

A paradox, too, is that people are wealthier, so they want more goods, but they have less time to spend it, so that makes it more important that stress and hassle are removed if they are to part with cash. People who are cash-rich but time-poor will pay close attention to time spent queuing.

Peek has identified 12 key stages the shopper goes through from leaving the comfort of the Saturday afternoon couch to returning home, which need to be "de-stressed" if "post-purchase dissonance" is to be removed.

Peek begins his work miles away from the site, since research indicates that women, whose independence and growing wealth make them key targets, associate litter, scary roundabouts and traffic jams miles away from the development with the whole negative experience.

Too many roundabouts, he has discovered, are stressful for women. At Bluewater no roundabout will have more than two exits, as more choices are perceived stressful and contrary to the lovely trance-like day-dream in which the company want their "guests" to arrive. Research also indicated that people wanted 25 per cent more space round their cars in that vast car park to manipulate push-chairs and trolleys.

Great thought at Bluewater went into flooring materials. Shiny surfaces are out, says Peek, because shiny means slippery and women are afraid of falling. Peek began with terrazzo tiles and a few small bits of York stone around the outside. He found that people inevitably gravitated towards natural materials.

Peek research has identified six consumer "types": Club Executives, County Classics, Young Fashionables, Young Survivors, Sporting 30s, Budget Optimists and Home Comfortables. Home Comfortables, he says, are pensioners or people who have stopped competing in their careers. They have gone home in a metaphoric sulk and want comfort and value, not aesthetics. Young Fashionables seem to lack analytical skills but know what they want when they see it and go for it voraciously.

Doesn't the great consumerist ever feel guilty about asking us to spend money we don't want to spend? Peek demurs: "I have a strong aversion to conning people. I believe that to earn money you must give outstanding value." That's a message he thinks that many British retailers might do well to ponder as the world slips into recession.

© *Telegraph Group Ltd., London 2000.*

Model Paper G

Questions on Passage 1

Marks

(a) How does the context help you to arrive at the meaning of "zenith" in line 1? — 2 U

(b) By careful analysis of word choice and sentence structure, explain how effectively the author creates a picture of the power of wealthy women in paragraph 1. — 4 E/A

(c) What contribution is made to the argument by the author's comments about musical comedies in paragraph 1 (lines 8–11)? — 2 U

(d) Explain how the imagery sets the atmosphere in lines 16–18? — 2 A

(e) "The Ritz of retiring rooms" (line 36). Comment on the effectiveness of this phrase in summing up the description of the Ladies' Room at Debenham & Freebody. — 3 E

(f) What does the address EVERYTHING LONDON (line 41) tell us about Harrods? — 1 U

(g) Why does the author suggest that Gordon Selfridge must have been speaking "sarcastically" in line 46? — 2 U

(h) Look at lines 59–69. Explain ONE example which shows that Gordon Selfridge understood shoppers' psychology. — 2 U

(i) How did the great stores of the early 20th century reflect social conditions at the time? — 4 U

(j) Look carefully at the last paragraph (lines 78–87). By commenting on sentence structure and word choice explain to what extent the writer has put across his ideas effectively. — 4 E/A

(k) Look again at lines 50–69. Explain briefly how Gordon Selfridge proved himself an innovator in the development of the great stores of the early 20th century. — 6 U

(32)

Questions on Passage 2

(l) Comment on the effectiveness of the language in the opening paragraph in catching the attention of the reader. — 4 E/A

(m) Why do you think Bluewater has been described as an "environmentalist's nightmare"? — 1 U

(n) What is the social change being described in lines 29–44 which Peek believes must be taken into account by those developing shopping centres in the late 20th century? — 2 U

Marks

(o) Explain how the sentence beginning "This, said Peek, is not as daft . . ." (line 39) acts as a link between paragraphs 10 and 11.   **2 A**

(p) Comment on the effectiveness of the phrase "cash-rich but time-poor" as it is used in line 46.   **1 A/E**

(q) Explain the thinking behind Peek's insistence that his work begins far away from the site of the actual shopping centre. Use examples from the passage to help your explanation.   **4 U**

(r) What do you understand by the phrase a "metaphoric sulk" as used in line 67?   **2 U**

(s) Comment on the effectiveness of one example of jargon in the passage.   **2 E/A**

   (18)

Question on Both Passages

(t) By referring to style and content, explain which articles gives the most interesting view of 20th century shopping habits. You should consider viewpoint, sentence structure, paragraphing, word choice, imagery, etc.   **10 E/A**

   (10)

Total = (60)

$A = 16\tfrac{1}{2}$

$U = 28$

$E = 15\tfrac{1}{2}$

MODEL PAPER H

HIGHER ENGLISH

Interpretation

NATIONAL QUALIFICATIONS

Time: 1 hour 30 minutes

You should attempt all questions.

The total value of the Paper is 60 marks.

INTERPRETATION

There are TWO passages and questions.

Read the passages carefully and then answer all the questions which follow. **Use your own words whenever possible and particularly when you are instructed to do so.**

You should read the passages to:

- understand what the writers have to say about the problems faced when trying to write a biography (**Understanding — U**);
- analyse the choice of language, imagery and structures to show how they convey their points of view and contribute to the impact of the article (**Analysis — A**);
- evaluate how effectively each writer has achieved his purpose (**Evaluation — E**).

A code letter (U, A, E) is used alongside each question to give some indication of the skills being assessed. The number of marks attached to each question will give some indication of the length and kind of answer required.

PASSAGE 1

Passage 1 is taken from the introduction to "The Art of Literary Biography", edited by John Batchelor. In this passage, Richard Holmes discusses the problems faced by those writing biographies. In Passage 2, taken from "The Craft of Literary Biography", edited by Jeffrey Meyers, Jeffrey Meyers is introducing a book of essays by people who have written biographies and he is discussing what he thinks are some of the best approaches to the task.

BIOGRAPHY: INVENTING THE TRUTH

What I want to suggest is that biography — the form that I have loved and struggled with for nearly thirty years — is essentially, and by its very origins, disreputable. Its genius, and indeed its very genealogy, is impure. It was relished and attacked during its first popular flowering in the eighteenth century, just as it is relished and attacked today.
5 It has always had the doubtful status of a maverick or mongrel art, and that is precisely why it remains so alive, so adaptable, so dangerous for all concerned: writers, subjects, readers, and most of all its critics who want it to behave.

Let me propose a simple myth of its genesis, a sort of Origin of the Species. The problematic, delightful, and disputed nature of biography derives from its original two
10 forebears, who one secret, sultry morning formed an Unholy Alliance. Fiction married Fact, without benefit of clergy. Or as I prefer to say, Invention formed a love-match with Truth. These are the Adam and Eve of our subject. The result was a brilliant, bastard form — Biography — which has been causing trouble ever since.

Consider for a moment the extraordinary divergence in the offspring produced. The two most successful biographies in the English language to date are probably James Boswell's "Life of Samuel Johnson" (1791), which has never been out of print for 200 years; and Andrew Morton's "Diana: Her True Story" (1992), "including a new chapter and 28 new photographs", which has sold two and a half million copies worldwide and whose sales will be clicking upwards as we annotate our footnotes.

The diversity of the biographic form, and range of inventive power with which it can render both the external details and the inward nature of life — its power to reconstruct and to intrude — have always posed certain problematic questions. I should like to raise four of these, which each reflect something of the controversial nature of the form we have inherited. They concern ethics, authenticity, celebrity, and the principle of empathy.

The ethics of research into another person's life have always been questionable. By what right, by what contract, does a biographer enter into another's zone of activity and privacy? Even an actual legal contract with a dead author's estate does not necessarily cover this issue. The idea of the biographer as a pursuing hound — James Joyce's "biografiend" — has been present from the start. Dr Arbuthnot, writing in the eighteenth century of the innumerable biographical pamphlets by the "unspeakable" Edmund Curll, gloomily remarked that biography had "added a new Terror to Death". Ian Hamilton has vividly dramatized the case in his study of J.D. Salinger, where the novelist resorts to law to defend his privacy. The long saga of Ted Hughes's battles against Sylvia Plath's biographers puts the question in its most anguished, immediate form.

Next there is the problem of authenticity. Biographers base their work on sources which are inherently unreliable. Memory itself is fallible; memoirs are inevitably biased; letters are always slanted towards their recipients; even private diaries and intimate journals have to be recognized as literary forms of self-invention rather than an "ultimate" truth of private fact or feeling. The biographer has always had to construct or orchestrate a factual pattern out of materials that already have a fictional or reinvented element. Perhaps the most insidious lies in the apparently established ground of earlier or "authorised works". A remarkable example appeared recently in Christopher Benfey's intriguing work "The Double Life of Stephen Crane" (1993), in which Benfey shows that Crane's early standard biography by Thomas Beer (1923) was in fact a tissue of invention.

Third comes the peculiar magnetism of celebrity. Biography has always been drawn towards the famous, the glamorous, the notorious. It is pulled, unnaturally perhaps, out of the orbit of the ordinary, the average, the everyday lives that most of us lead and need to understand. Instead it typically tells the stories of great saints and great sinners; kings, actors, criminals, generals, Romantic poets, mad novelists. There are over 200 lives of Lord Byron. The "minor" character, the faithful spouse, the loyal companion, the intelligent sensible friend, are so often reduced to footnotes, the unmarked grave at the foot of the page. This can be seen as a fundamental distortion within the form's capacity to deal with life in its largest, broadest sense as we mostly experience it. Freud defined this as the problem of "hero worship" inherent in the genre, with its concomitant but suppressed desire to devalue greatness, to find the feet of clay and the rattling skeleton in the cupboard.

Biography finds it difficult to deal imaginatively with the mundane. And where the mundane, in its richest sense, is central to a life — as in a happy marriage, or a long and constant friendship — it is often peculiarly impotent, both in its source (what house companions write letters to each other?) and in its narrative invention (how to describe twenty years of tender, ruminative breakfasts?).

Lastly, there is the complicated and subtle question of empathy. Why is a biographer drawn to particular subjects, what element of suppressed autobiography is involved, and how does this affect the possibilities of an "objectively" truthful account? I have tried to examine some of these delicate, self reflexive issues in a book called "Footsteps" (1985), but I am still deeply puzzled and fascinated by them. The power of certain lives to draw endlessly repeated reassessments — Johnson, Byron, Napoleon, Queen Victoria, D.H. Lawrence, Plath — is a peculiar mystery. It suggests that they hold particular mirrors up to each succeeding generation of biographers, almost as the classical myths were endlessly retold by the Greek dramatists, to renew their own versions of contemporary identity. Each generation sees itself anew in its chosen subjects.

Let me end by emphasising, as I began, that for all its problems — of ethics, authenticity, celebrity, and empathy — this seems to me the most *lovable* of modern English literary forms. If I had to define biography in a single phrase, I would call it an art of human understanding, and a celebration of human nature. We should, I am sure, be proud of it.

(Richard Holmes)

PASSAGE 2

Introduction

Biography has become one of the major literary genres of the twentieth century. There is now considerable interest not only in the history of life writing but also in how a biography comes into being, how the biographer captures the essence of an artist's inner life. "The Craft of Literary Biography" describes the problems of writing a modern
5 literary biography from thirteen different viewpoints. It considers, among many other questions, how the biographer chooses a subject, uses biographical models, does archival research, conducts interviews, interprets evidence, establishes chronology, organizes material into a meaningful pattern and illuminates an author's work through a discussion of his life.

10 The ideal circumstances for selecting a modern literary subject are the existence of significant unpublished material, of family and friends who can be interviewed as well as the absence of an obstructive executor. Most contemporary readers expect to learn the whole truth about the psychological, sexual and medical aspects of the subject. For this reason, writers like Kafka, Eliot, Orwell and Auden vainly tried to protect their
15 posthumous privacy by requesting that no biography be written about them. Auden asserted that "Biographies of writers, whether written by others or by themselves, are always superfluous and usually in bad taste . . . His private life is, or should be, of no concern to anybody except himself, his family and his friends." But Samuel Johnson's belief (expressed in "The Rambler" of October 13, 1750), "There has rarely passed a
20 life of which a judicious and faithful narrative would not be useful," has prevailed from his time until our own.

The traditional aim of the literary biographer — to discover, define and depict the mind as well as the life of the artist — has been rejected by a superficial school of life writing, which prefers to present an external view through an encyclopaedic accumulation of
25 facts. The predictable result of this is a clumsy style, an absence of interpretation and a lack of perception. These books fail to present a convincing and meaningful pattern in the author's life; an exploration of character, an evaluation of relationships, a comprehension of motives.

The more ambitious and successful biographer is an investigative reporter of the spirit.
30 He must reveal evolution and development, present the numerous selves and multiple lives of his subject; for as Henry James observed: "To live over people's lives is nothing unless we live over their perceptions, live over the growth, the change, the varying intensity of the same — since it was *by* these things they themselves lived." The literary biographer must utilise original research that casts new light on the subject; have a
35 thorough mastery of the material; give a complete and accurate synthesis of all the facts about the private as well as the public life: friendships, conversations, dress, habits, tastes, food, money. He should make a selection — not merely a collection — of significant and convincing details, and possess a lively narrative style. He should form a sympathetic identification with the subject, and present a perceptive interpretation of
40 character. He must create a dramatic structure that focuses the pattern of crises in the life, and effectively portray the social and political background. He ought to provide a sensitive evaluation of the subject's achievement — which is the justification of the book. Finally, as Somerset Maughan (who was trained as a doctor) noted, he must also do justice to the end and extinction of the life: "In most biographies it is the subject's

death which is most interesting. The last inevitable step has a fascination and even a practical interest which no previous event can equal. I cannot understand why a biographer, having undertaken to give the world details of a famous man's life, should hesitate, as so often happens, to give details of his death."

Modern biography reached its peak in the 1950s with an impressive series of monumental works; most notably, George Painter's "Marcel Proust" (2 volumes, 1959, 1965) and Richard Ellmann's "James Joyce" (1959, revised edition 1982). Painter and Ellmann, who have influenced most subsequent literary biographies, fulfil the ideal of sympathetic intuition and recreate the subjects' lives by intimately reliving (as James suggested) their perceptions, their growth and their change. Through this essential process and with great psychological penetration, both beautifully written biographies reveal how these two major novelists were drawn to their literary vocation — to the religion of art.

Several significant themes emerge from the essays which follow: the change from paralysis when faced with the apparently overwhelming task to a moment of insight and a confident conviction that one can successfully complete the book; the need to replace myth with facts; the joy of detection and discovery; the reliance on help from others and importance of (well-deserved) luck; the creative process that demands the same imaginative qualities as fiction and drama; the struggle to preserve the integrity of their work when confronted with the compromising expediency of publishers. All the biographers attempted to define themselves while exploring the lives of their subjects, placing them in the proper context and illuminating their art. The contributors to "The Craft of Literary Biography", who present a retrospective view of their own works as well as a penetrating analysis of the state of contemporary biography, confirm Lytton Strachey's observation: "It is perhaps as difficult to write a good life as to live one."

(Jeffrey Meyers)

Model Paper H

Questions on Passage 1

Marks

(a) By careful analysis of the word choice and sentence structure in lines 1–7, explain how the author supports his view that Biography is "disreputable". — 4 A

(b) To what extent do you find the way the writer develops the image of "The Origin of the Species" in the second paragraph (lines 8–13) effective? — 4 A/E

(c) What purpose does the last sentence in paragraph 4 (lines 24–25) "They concern . . ." have in the passage as a whole? — 2 A

(d) Show how the context of paragraph 5, lines 26–36, makes clear what James Joyce meant by his coined word "biografiend" in line 30. — 2 U

(e) Explain TWO of the problems facing a biographer in his search for the truth about his subject? — 4 U

(f) Look carefully at lines 56–59. Explain the underlying paradox which Freud recognized in the attitudes of those writing (or reading) biography. — 2 U

(g) What do you think the writer meant by "Each generation sees itself anew in its chosen subjects" (lines 74–75)? — 2 U

(h) How effective do you find the sentence structure of the last sentence in expressing the conclusion of this article? — 2 A/E

(22)

Questions on Passage 2

(i) (i) Look at paragraph 1, lines 5–9. From the information in this paragraph, how would you sum up the nature of a biography writer's work? — 1 U

(ii) Show how the writer has used word choice and sentence structure to help create this impression. — 4 A

(j) In your own words, explain three main requirements, suggested by the writer, in choosing a subject for a good modern biography. — 3 U

(k) Look carefully at paragraph 2. What are the two opposing views of those who may have biographies written about them? — 2 U

(l) Look carefully at the last sentence of paragraph 3 (line 26, "These books fail . . ."). Explain how the sentence structure helps to put forward his opinion. — 2 A

Marks

(m) Explain how lines 29–33 help you to arrive at the meaning of the phrase "an investigative reporter of the spirit" as used in line 29.

2 U

(n) Why do you think the writer has included the aside about Somerset Maughan in line 43 "(who was trained as a doctor)" in paragraph 4 ?

2 U

(o) Look at the word choice and imagery in paragraph 5 (lines 49–57). Explain the extent to which you think the writer has expressed his perception of two good biographies effectively.

4 A/E

(p) Think about the ideas expressed in this introduction. Do you think the quotation by Lytton Strachey used as a final comment makes a good ending?

2 E/U

(q) Look again at paragraph 5 (lines 49–57). Explain as briefly as possible what a good biographer must do to produce a successful biography.

6 U

(28)

Questions on Both Passages

(r) Look again at both passages. Which one seems to you to raise the most interesting ideas about the problems inherent in the writing of biography?

4 E

(s) Which of the two writers presents his comments on the writing of biographies in the more interesting and clearer way?

6 E/A

(10)

Total = (60)

A = 20

U = 27

E = 13

NOTES

ACKNOWLEDGEMENTS

We are extremely grateful to the following for permission to use copyright material in this book.

Story of the Wreck of the Titanic
by Marshall Everett.
Reprinted by permission of the Publisher, Conway Maritime Press.

Article on Petra
by Don Belt.
Reprinted by permission of the Publisher, National Geographic Society.

A History of Lighthouses
Reprinted by permission of the Author, Patrick Beaver.

Extract from *Lighthouses and Lightships*
by Lee Chadwick.
Published by Dobson Books Ltd.

Article from 'The Scotsman' — *Tartan myth by design*
by J.B. Pick.
Reprinted by permission of the Author, J.B. Pick.

Extract from *Robert the Bruce*
by Ronald McNair Scott.
Reprinted by permission of the Publisher,
Canongate Books Ltd, 14 High Street, Edinburgh, EH1 1TE.

Hot Air Ballooning © 1978
by Dick Brown.
Published, Tab Books.
Reproduced with permission of The McGraw-Hill Companies.

Extract from *Richard Branson: The Inside Story*
by Mick Brown © 1988.
First Published by Michael Joseph Ltd., 1988.
Reproduced by permission of Penguin Books Ltd.

Article from 'The Scotsman' — *Be afraid. Be very afraid.*
by Trevor Johnston.
Reprinted by permission of the Publisher, The Scotsman Publications Ltd.

Extract from *BFI Modern Classics — The Exorcist*
by Mark Kermode.
Reprinted by permission of The British Film Institute.

Extract from *Shops and Shopping 1800–1914* (© 1964)
by Alison Adburgham.
Published by George Allen and Unwin Ltd.
Reprinted by permission of Mr. R. Adburgham

Extract from 'The Daily Telegraph' — *Persuading Us To Shop Till We Drop*
by Charles Clover.
© Telegraph Group Ltd., London 2000.

Extract from *The Art of Literary Biography* (© 1995)
Edited by John Batchelor.
Reprinted by permission of the Publisher, Oxford University Press.

Extract from *The Craft of Literary Biography* (© 1985)
Edited by Jeffrey Meyers.
Reprinted by permission of the Publisher, Macmillan Ltd.

Printed by Bell & Bain Ltd., Glasgow, Scotland.